PATH OF RESISTANCE
THE PRACTICE OF CIVIL DISOBEDIENCE

by
PER HERNGREN

translated by
MARGARET RAINEY

NEW SOCIETY PUBLISHERS
Philadelphia, PA   Gabriola Island, BC

English-language edition © 1993 by Per Herngren.
All rights reserved.

Inquiries regarding requests to reprint all or part of *Path of Resistance: The Practice of Civil Disobedience* should be addressed to:
New Society Publishers
4527 Springfield Avenue
Philadelphia, PA 19143

ISBN USA 0-86571-252-2 Hardcover
ISBN USA 0-86571-253-0 Paperback
ISBN CAN 1-55092-194-0 Hardcover
ISBN CAN 1-55092-195-9 Paperback

Translated from the Swedish by Margaret Rainey.

Printed in the United States of America on partially recycled paper with soy ink by Capital City Press of Montpelier, Vermont.

Cover art by Larry Nolte.
Cover design by Nancy Adams.
Book design by Martin Kelley.

To order directly from the publisher, add $2.50 to the price for the first copy, 75¢ each additional. Send check or money order to:
New Society Publishers
4527 Springfield Avenue
Philadelphia, PA 19143
In Canada, contact:
New Society Publishers/New Catalyst
PO Box 189
Gabriola Island, BC VOR 1XO

New Society Publishers is a project of the New Society Educational Foundation, a nonprofit, tax-exempt, public foundation in the United States, and of the Catalyst Education Society, a non-profit society in Canada. Opinions expressed in this book do not necessarily represent positions of the New Society Educational Foundation, nor the Catalyst Education Society.

® GCIU

Under a government which imprisons any unjustly, the true place for a just man is also in prison.

— Henry David Thoreau,
"Civil Disobedience," 1849

CONTENTS

PUBLISHER'S NOTE

I remember the first time I came across a path of resistance—I stumbled onto it actually. It was the last leg of a transcontinental peace walk, and as I travelled my precious two weeks with it, I absorbed all I could of its culture. Along those roads, I found people organized around ideals that I was only beginning to grasp in my own intensely-private and personal searchings. While I had struggled to carve a small (and lonely) niche for myself, here were wondrous people coming together to build communities in which we might all hope to find shelter.

Alongside the roads, I saw people supporting each other in the acts of conscience and of life in which they engaged. I came to recognize a loosely-knit, sometimes-quarrelsome, but always-fascinating family of peace activists, who had come together that year to dream, toil, play, and sometimes cry with one another as they built a more peaceful and loving world.

How surprised I was to learn that this motley band had many histories and many stories, which together created a diverse and rich culture! They were part of an ongoing peace movement, with a long and proud history. While I had sat at home trying to reinvent all sorts of wheels, here was a culture, history, and people with whom I could travel and learn.

Since those heady two weeks, I have come to appreciate even more deeply the communities of peace into which we can root ourselves. And I have been fortunate enough to find a space where I can both listen to and pass along the stories of my fellow walkers for peace.

* * *

When I first met Per Herngren, he was perched over a handheld tape recorder, coaxing just these kind of stories from a lifelong sojourner of the peace movement. Into a small Dutch monastery had gathered an international assemblage of fifty nonviolent activists to share and learn from each other's experiences, and Per was there collecting stories of lives lived along paths of resistance.

The book you hold in your hands is a distillation of these and many other tales. Per has travelled across three continents, all the while tasting the local forms of resistance and cataloguing the ingredients for communities of peace. He has boiled all of this down into a stew of collective wisdom, and flavored it with his own experiences opposing militarism, both here in North America and in his native Scandinavia. Here are recipes—cook them to taste—for lives of resistance.

Bon apetit and happy trails to you!

Martin Kelley

Martin Kelley
for New Society Publishers
January 23, 1993

INTRODUCTION:
A HANDBOOK IS BORN

One of my first lessons in civil disobedience came when my brother was born. He was a glowing red package that arrived on my twelfth birthday. At first I refused to even touch this fragile creature. Then I carefully picked him up. After a while I could sit for hours with David in my arms. His uncomplicated assertion of will fascinated me: when something was wrong, he simply refused to cooperate. I was, on the other hand, a very obedient son.

Don't get me wrong. I don't mean that I never protested. I protested wildly. I screamed and argued. But when everything was said and done, I obeyed anyway. The contrast between me and my brother has helped me to understand clearly the difference between resistance and protest. Today "resistance" is a fashionable word, and all types of protest are suddenly being called resistance. This is unfortunate. Resistance is disobedience. Protest can in some situations be more appropriate, but it is not the same as resistance (though under a dictatorship, even a protest can be illegal and can therefore become a form of resistance).

Many years later, when I had a few years of prison ahead of me because I had disarmed nuclear weapons components in a Plowshares action, I finally came to understand the full challenge in my brother's behavior. Earlier, I had skimmed through my father's Martin Luther King collection. By taking courses in civil disobedience, I tried to learn what I could about current discussions on the subject. I participated in several actions against Swedish arms exports and against the new nuclear weapons that the Soviet Union had placed in Europe. In order to get more firsthand experience I moved to the U.S.

All of this education was necessary in order to understand how deeply obedience was rooted in me and how difficult it is to overcome. After being moved among about ten different prisons in the U.S. during the period of a year, I realized how vitally important the struggle against obedience is. We must struggle with fear; we must struggle with ourselves.When I confronted my own fear, I realized that disobedience isn't a leisure-time activity. It is a lifelong task for each and every one of us. When I faced the personal consequences of my disobedience, I felt I had touched the central nerve of our modern society: our self-imposed obedience.

In this handbook, I have tried to write about how to resist obedience in a practical way. During the first few years of my life, as I saw in my baby brother, resistance was probably a natural reaction. But through contact with other people, I learned to obey. Today I need to learn how to overcome obedience.This book is about that process.

During my time in jail, I decided to write a civil disobedience handbook. I had collected a dozen different handbooks from the U.S., England, and India. Primarily written before actions, these handbooks were excerpts about the most fundamental experiences in how to organize and carry out civil disobedience. But these handbooks were *too* elementary for my broader purposes. There is a lot of experience within the nonviolence movement. However, this experience is communicated mainly in discussions or other kinds of personal contacts between individuals. Nobody seems to have taken the time to write this collective experience down. This handbook is an attempt to get recent experience in nonviolence down on paper. I discuss the past few years of organizing actions through sections on affinity groups, retreats, training, advanced forms of democracy, etc. Each and every one of these subjects could fill a book, but this treatment is, in any case, more comprehensive than other books written on the subject. My intent is that this handbook will be useful for a variety of situations, including support work for refugees, solidarity work with the Third World, protection of the environment, disarmament, furthering the demands of disabled citizens, and struggles for labor rights. This book is a discussion about contemporary, hands-on civil disobedience that has, up until now, occurred only among activists. Civil disobedience has developed and changed radically during the past few years. Resistance during the nineties will hopefully profit by the mistakes of the past. It is important to continue to develop civil disobedience; otherwise, resistance will become only a marginal political phenomenon.

This handbook is divided into nine chapters. The first chapter introduces the idea of civil disobedience in a democracy, the ethical prerequisites for resistance, a definition of civil disobedience, and the importance of nonviolence. The rest of the book discusses actions of civil disobedience, focusing on the practical and ethical difficulties and potential of the different stages of an action—from preparations, to the choice of a particular action, to the trial, to punishment for the action.

The second chapter is an overview of the preparations necessary before an action: establishing an affinity group, preparing the action itself, and doing research. It begins with a historical and philosophical summary of the importance of conflict in the creation of a resistance community, and the importance of this community in the fight against fear of punishment. It then discusses the dynamics and responsibilities of affinity groups and how the group can research the information needed for an action. Chapter 3 deals with different kinds of civil disobedience one might choose to do, such as the Sanctuary movement's experiences in hiding refugees and my experiences with the Plowshares movement's disarmament actions. Conscientious objection, blockades, and other types of actions are also discussed. The fourth chapter describes how to organize actions. It focuses primarily on the possibilities of starting a dialogue using arrest, interrogation, and other communication channels.

Trial and punishment are often mistakenly viewed as unfortunate consequences of civil disobedience. For this reason, the importance of each of these factors in the fight against our passivity is discussed in two separate chapters, 5 and 6. The trial provides an opportunity to start a dialogue. If the trial results in a prison sentence or fines, then new possibilities for resistance are created. Chapter 7 explains the new democratic tools used throughout the peace and alternative movements. The development of democratic methods intensified during the seventies and eighties. Therefore, this chapter presents experience with the new tools for democracy, mediation techniques, and consensus decisionmaking. My intent is to describe methods that undermine both hierarchical power structures and oppression. The final chapter contains my reflections about the future and the possibilities created by civil disobedience.

This handbook should not be read as a set of detailed instructions about how you should deal with any particular situation. Rather, it is the responsibility of the reader to utilize these experiences and synthesize them into new actions that will challenge obedience to an even greater extent.

CHAPTER I

THE PATH OF RESISTANCE: ABOUT CIVIL DISOBEDIENCE

WHAT IS CIVIL DISOBEDIENCE?

Disobedience is nothing new. *Civil disobedience*, however, is a fairly new phenomenon. The idea of civil disobedience first came from the American writer Henry David Thoreau, and was argued in his classic essay, "Civil Disobedience," published in 1849.[1] As a protest against slavery, oppression, and the U.S. war against Mexico, he refused to pay war taxes. Refusal to pay taxes was not a new idea: it was used by anti-slavery abolitionists, among others. Karl Marx had also tried to organize a campaign to convince people to refuse to pay taxes during the revolution in Europe in 1848. The originality in Thoreau's idea was that he insisted that society react. Thoreau saw civil disobedience as a whole entity, where punishment was at least as important as the action of breaking the law. This made civil disobedience a very special form of action. Punishment—or overcoming the power of punishment—is the very foundation of civil disobedience. Thoreau had asserted that "action from principle, the perception and the performance of right," is above the law, and fundamentally revolutionary.[2] A country's government is powerless without the cooperation and obedience of its citizens. Mahatma Gandhi, who led the struggle against English colonialism in India, demonstrated concretely that massive disobedience can render the state power ineffective. "If man will only realize that it is unmanly to obey laws that are unjust, no man's tyranny will enslave him," Gandhi said.[3]

This brings us to another original aspect of Thoreau. His resistance was directed toward obedient citizens, not toward the government which instigated what he saw as unjust deeds. It was citizens that made and make up the most important target group for civil disobedience. Thoreau considered the "most conscientious supporters" of injustice and "the most serious obstacles" to reform to be the people, those who, in spite of being opposed to the government, "yield to it their allegiance and support."[4] He assumed that there were enough people to put a stop to war and slavery if they moved from having opinions to active disobedience.

The problem is, however, that most of us are obedient. But when some people accept the consequences of disobedience by doing civil disobedience, others are challenged to break unjust laws and decisions. In this way, they show us, as Thoreau showed us, that one of the obstacles to creating a just world—fear of personal consequences—can be overcome.

A Definition of Civil Disobedience

Civil disobedience has developed from liberal and humanist traditions. People who have honestly grappled with the dilemma of modern democracies have tried civil disobedience as a democratic means for minorities and other groups that are oppressed to obtain justice (though not just Western democracies, but also dictatorships in the Third

World and socialist one-party countries have been confronted with civil disobedience). The dynamic of the method is based on the very foundation of democracy—the dialogue. Civil disobedience functions only because of its democratic dynamic. Keeping this conversation about right action going is essential to seeing an unjust law overturned. This principle of dialogue is one difference between this method and methods that are directly effective, like boycott, strike, disobedience on a massive scale, or direct action. These methods can also improve democracy, but function above all as a means of creating political pressure.

What is the role of civil disobedience in a democracy? In his now classic book, *A Theory of Justice* from 1971, John Rawls examines the role of civil disobedience in a "nearly just regime."[5] According to Rawls, civil disobedience is not difficult to justify in an unjust regime, that is in a country whose government does not follow the will of the majority. Problems arise, however, in a nearly just regime. His theory implies that those who practice civil disobedience belong to a minority that has turned against the will of the majority

According to Rawls, it is not possible to justify civil disobedience by pleading religious or private views. Instead, one must appeal to the society's sense of justice. He assumes that in a nearly just regime the citizens have a general understanding of justice. Civil disobedience then provides a minority with a method that makes the majority reflect upon whether the validity of the act of civil disobedience is in accordance with its sense of justice or not. An action functions in this case as an appeal.

He emphasizes that it is up to the individual to decide when it is right to practice civil disobedience. Each and every person is responsible for his or her actions. This does not mean that we can make any decision we want to. To be a responsible citizen means to heed the political principles that make up the legal foundation for our kind of democracies. Civil disobedience is, writes Rawls, an action that is public, nonviolent, conscientious, political, and illegal. The goal of civil disobedience is usually to change the law or change a government's decision. An action appeals to the majority's sense of justice, and its message is that the principles of social cooperation between free and equal people have not been respected. Rawls makes even one more distinction, that "direct" civil disobedience should be aimed at the law that is broken. It is this law that must change. "Indirect" civil disobedience, on the other hand, is aimed at a different law or decision from the one that should change.

I use a definition that is both more general and yet somewhat narrower than Rawls's definition. This is my definition:

- Civil disobedience is a public action.
- It is based on nonviolence.
- The action is illegal or defies a command or decision.
- The direct intent of the action is to preserve or change a phenomenon in the society.
- The personal consequences of the action are an important part of the message.

"Civil" usually means pertaining to the citizen. In the nonviolence movement, "civil" has a more narrow definition. Civil is, in this context, the opposite of violence. Those who do acts of civil disobedience behave in a civilized manner, with respect for the opponent as a person. By "opponent" I mean discussion partner, the one the action is directed towards. Discussion partners at one action can be representatives of the law and at another the owners of a company.

My definition is broader than Rawls's definition in the sense that I do not include, as he does, the demand that one must have a serious personal conviction. I am interested in an action that has a special political dynamic. I do not see any reason to include a judgment of an activist's psyche and consciousness in a definition. Civil disobedience is civil disobedience even if a few doubters participate. Just like the believers, they can start a dialogue during a trial about what is right and wrong.

Another difference between our definitions is that Rawls differentiates between conscientious objection and civil disobedience. Conscientious objection is when one defies a decision or command for reasons of conscience. It is then, argues Rawls, more of a private moral action than a political action. But open conscientious objection at a place of work has political consequences. According to my definition, conscientious objection can also be civil disobedience, if the other criteria have been filled.

In a public action, the participants do not try to avoid the consequences of the action. Therefore, painting an anonymous political message on a wall under cover of darkness is not civil disobedience—though, in itself, painting messages on walls can be a good thing even if it isn't civil disobedience!

Disobedience can be illegal according to one law and legal according to another. Martin Luther King's and the North American civil rights movement's resistance to racist state laws is one example. In several cases their actions were supported by federal laws. The Plowshares movement's disarmament of weapons is also a good example of this. During the trials afterwards, we state that the weapons we disarm are illegal according to international law—the Numemberg Principles, for instance—and we are, in accordance with that law, bound to protest.[6]

Civil disobedience is always a political act. It exceeds the personal interests of the participants. Some people therefore do not define *private* deeds as civil disobedience. Personal interest can, however, in many cases be the primary interest.

A friend of mine was awakened one morning when her bedroom was engulfed by a cloud of dust. The company that owned the apartment building had begun to renovate the apartment next door. My friend refused to pay the rent and demanded restitution. The landlord agreed to her demands. She was paid restitution and did not have to pay the rent for that month. Even if the struggle she had was private, it still was about her rights as a tenant. That is why it exceeded her personal interests and can be defined as civil disobedience. *Civil resistance* was for a long time a synonym of civil disobedience. Today, however, it is used mainly to indicate civil disobedience in time of war against invasion or coup. *Holy* or *divine obedience* is used in about the same way as civil disobedience.

At first, Gandhi used the expression *"passive resistance"* with about the same meaning as *nonviolent resistance*. This expression is not as popular today, since the word "passive" gives the wrong associations.

As I mentioned earlier, resistance means disobedience or refusal. It is a wide concept and could be used for everything from military defense to my baby brother's refusal to eat his dinner. Resistance is not necessarily always a good thing. It can be destructive. Even nonviolent resistance is not always positive, and neither is civil disobedience. Those that believe that civil disobedience is always right place the *method* above the consideration of people's wants and needs. Just like any other act, one must judge disobedience according to the *intent* and the *way* in which it is done. Neither the political *results* nor the use of the right *method* can justify an action's negative consequences for people.

The Differences Between
Civil Disobedience and Direct Action

Civil disobedience as a method is not intended primarily to influence public opinion but is, above all, a way of challenging others to be disobedient. The action alone cannot achieve this. Only in combination with punishment does the action become a true challenge of obedience. Of course, it is not possible to maintain that Thoreau's special method is always the best one. Civil disobedience is quite simply a method that can be useful in certain historical contexts to achieve certain goals.

A group like the environmental organization Greenpeace, for instance, maintains that they do not use civil disobedience, in spite of the fact that many of their actions are illegal. When Greenpeace activists hang onto the railing of a ship that intends to dump waste in the sea, the action's political effect is important. The action should, with the help of the mass media, influence the decisionmakers. Greenpeace's method could be called "direct action."

Direct action means that the end becomes the means. This can be done symbolically, as when the peace movement in Sweden began to seriously work against arms exports in 1983. We were a loosely connected group of peace workers that stopped an arms ship. By preventing the export of arms for an hour, we wanted to point symbolically to our goal of stopping all arms exports. Direct action can also mean the realization of a goal. Homeless people that occupy a house have realized one of their goals. Starting a store that sells products that are bought directly from cooperatives in the Third World is an example of a lawful direct action. Such a store creates a new economic order on a small scale.

Most direct actions also work indirectly and symbolically because they influence decisionmakers and others. For Greenpeace a strong indirect effect is the point of a direct action. They achieve this indirect effect by showing what needs to be done. When activists hang onto the railing, they physically stop the ship from dumping wastes on them and into the sea. Symbolic actions do not exclude the use of symbols of *force*. Christian activists in England have for some strange reason gone head over heels for chains. They chain themselves to the gates of military bases, for example. This is not done to achieve a goal by the strength of the chains, but to get their message out to the public.

In the U.S., a conflict arose at the end of the sixties between those that advocated direct physical action and those that advocated civil disobedience. A similar debate is going on in Europe today. Some groups in the women's movement, for example, maintain that attempts at *physically effective* resistance led to a "terror balance" based on physical strength, which excluded large groups from the struggle. Nonviolence here becomes an elitist phenomenon. My own criticism of *physical* resistance is that it is useful only in a certain historical situation, namely when so many people participate in a protest that the authorities are not willing to use sufficient resources to stop it. They choose instead to negotiate. However, we have not come that far yet. To stop the manufacturing of weapons with effective actions, several thousand people would probably have to participate.

Until we have come that far, disobedience will mostly be useful to mobilize resistance and to start dialogue. Even during a growing mass resistance, discussions with the opponent will still be important. Democracy is based on the assumption that all parties involved come to an agreement. Resistance should be based on the conditions for democracy.

Another risk with *physically effective* resistance is that this way of thinking creates a certain frustration if it fails. The result can be an unnecessary misdirected struggle that is mostly with the police, which leads to actions whose symbolism damages the struggle. The actions become simply a support for the opponent's behavior and an obstacle stopping others from becoming active. Instead of a useful direct action where the end becomes the means, a struggle to show who is physically strongest risks becoming its negation—the means become the end. This is the breeding ground for violence.

Civil disobedience depends on direct contact with those that support the system. In order to carry on a dialogue, actions and trials are necessary. By some taking the consequences of their actions, others are encouraged to do likewise.

THE METHOD OF THE ETHICS

Civil disobedience can best be seen as a dialogue. It is a dialogue with the opponent through actions and trials, and a dialogue with other citizens based on the challenge that the punishment signifies. This discussion is about two subjects: what is possible and impossible, and what is right and wrong.

During an unsuccessful attempt at party politics when I was a teenager, I saw how the questions of what is right and what is possible were separated. Nonviolence does quite the opposite, according to its tradition. Here ethics and the given conditions are closely connected. This is not a harmonious, conflict-free relationship, but it is a relationship nevertheless. Resistance is based on both conditions.

To a certain extent we allow others to control our behavior due to our interpretation of what is generally perceived as being possible. Through our actions we either confirm or change this general perception. For example, it is considered self-evident that only governments in disarmament negotiations can decide which weapons should be destroyed. When workers at a weapons factory or other people suddenly start disarming weapons on their own, our view of what is possible and of who can act changes.

Our behavior is also governed by our interpretation of what is generally viewed as being right. Through our actions, we confirm or change this outlook. To obey the law and to not destroy property are two moral principles embedded in our culture. When environmental activists disassemble machines that destroy the environment, and the law protects the destruction of nature, these two principles are confronted with each other in complex ways and we have the possibility of increasing our understanding of what is right and wrong.

In order to keep the dialogue going so that one side did not become quiet or blocked, Gandhi used a method when practicing resistance that can be compared to climbing a staircase. This meant that a campaign should begin with negotiations and escalate, first with protest, then boycott, noncooperation, and civil disobedience, and if all of this did not help, parallel rule and alternative institutions should be established. During the well-known salt march when Indians broke the English colonial laws and started extracting salt from seawater, a journalist asked Gandhi what he would do if the authorities did not react. "Then I have to escalate the campaign," was the answer.

The opponent's reactions are a necessary part of resistance, whether they make concessions or put people in jail. Yet this is not because the opponent shows its true nature through its reactions, as some guerrilla groups claim. With actions, the opponent shows only its standpoint, which is something changeable. By forcing a reaction, the whole society, with its officials and citizens, is drawn into a dialogue.

The dialogue should not be allowed to cease because the struggle stops at a certain level and is ignored. However, the discussion can be silenced because of the opposite mistake. It is only the strong and clever that can go up a staircase with big steps. For fearless activists to hurry on ahead can destroy the possibility of a dialogue, though when people feel blocked, it is seldom because the struggle has escalated too fast. Many bad actions are more an expression of the participants' frustration than a sincere attempt to establish contact with an opponent.

Sometimes it can be less controversial to do civil disobedience that leads to a long punishment than actions that only lead to low fines. There are two reasons for this. At an action where the risks are small for the participants, the interest is too concentrated on the action itself. At stronger actions with correspondingly harder punishments, many more people question the authorities' reactions and standpoint—assuming of course that the action is perceived as being consistent and morally correct. At actions that do not have any significant legal consequences, furthermore, the participants tend to try to make the action stronger by behaving provocatively to accentuate the difference between the activists' and the authorities' standpoints. But there are better ways to start a dialogue than just acting provocatively.

The Ethics of the Method

Civil disobedience is not putting oneself above the law. Even when a law is broken, it is not ignored. The participants in an action do not sneak away from the consequences of the action. Civil disobedience is a political act that confronts the law and claims a higher perception and performance of justice. To claim a higher value than the law does not mean that one knows what the truth is. It is just a starting point for a dialogue. Hopefully, an agreement can be reached. This claiming of higher value has often been successful, for example in the development of the right to strike and freedom of religion.

Sometimes it is necessary to put oneself above the law. Then you are not choosing civil disobedience, but another method that is more suitable. When a refugee risks persecution if he or she is deported, for example, then civil disobedience is not always usable. Hiding the refugee becomes largely a humane act, which has political consequences only when those hiding refugees can publicly expose their activities. Only when a group discusses it openly can its activity be called civil disobedience.

What gives us the right to break the law?

To claim the individual's right to obey his or her conscience can be problematic, depending on how the concept is defined. If conscience is seen as an individual's private conviction then it can become a justification for any action. Thoreau begins his discussion of conscience and how we know what is right by asserting that a person has a fundamental responsibility toward his or her fellow beings. We should not subject anyone to injustice. In his book *Walden*, he indicates the rights of nature and animals as well. Thoreau lays the foundation for the possibility to do civil disobedience within our understanding of what is truly right. He even claims that it is our obligation to do what we perceive is right. He thinks that conscience is something that is outside of the individual's private convictions. This can be interpreted as a *common knowledge* of what is right and wrong.

Gandhi thought that the truth was absolute. But he claimed that our perception of truth changes. Nobody can have absolute knowledge of what is right. Conscience is decided by the historical situation and the individual's own experiences. Civil disobedience becomes a radical interpretation of the morals of the current society. Through dialogue during the trial, these morals are tested in relationship to the opponent's view. As long as resistance is done openly, other people are also challenged to take part in this dialogue. This dialogue prevents the resistance group from developing in a sectarian way and creating their own peculiar morality due to isolation.

Civil disobedience is effective only if it functions as a moral challenge. That is why civil disobedience is ineffective for immoral purposes, or more exactly purposes that are generally perceived as being wrong. Of course, there are examples of bad civil disobedience. When resistance groups block the possibility of a dialogue they strengthen and confirm the opponent's power. This can be perceived as a negative dialogue: the possibilities for citizens to understand and give their opinion are reduced with each action, and support for the opponent is increased. However, if the opponent for purely tactical reasons breaks off a dialogue, then this can increase the possibility for the resistance group to create a dialogue directly with other citizens. This development is, as a matter of fact, the most common. When the opponent sees that silence reduces its influence and power, then the chances for a fruitful dialogue increase again. Silence on the part of the opponent can therefore be viewed as an important element in the dialogue. This should, however, not be confused with a negative dialogue that arises when the resistance group blocks the possibility for dialogue.

We see here how the circle closes. Civil disobedience weaves together ethics and method; you cannot entirely separate one from the other.

Nonviolence

It is not just ends and means or ethics and methods that are connected to each other. Disobedience also has a direct relationship with obedience. It does not avoid that which it is struggling against; rather, disobedience presupposes obedience. One cannot understand people's obedience if there are not others that disobey. In the same way, nonviolence always has a direct relationship to violence. Nonviolence is a confrontation, a negation. It isn't appropriate to call distribution of flyers or demonstrations nonviolence—at least not in democratic countries—because they do not presuppose violence. Similarly, we cannot understand violence if there are not others that practice nonviolence. The concept of nonviolence is used above all in three different kinds of situations: in civil disobedience where the activists expect to be arrested; to describe a peaceful way to defend oneself against violence; and in attempts to reduce violence within one's own organization.

Gandhi used *satyagraha* as a complement to nonviolence. *Satya*, which means "truth," comes from *sat,* which in turn means being. *Agraha* means "holding on to." Gandhi used *agraha* as a synonym for "force." Satyagraha is then *truth-force.*[7] According to Gandhi, since no one can entirely know what the truth is, one cannot use violence to force the truth on others. Satyagraha is instead patience and sympathy. Patience means self-suffering.[8] Civil disobedience is therefore a necessary part of satyagraha.

Today nonviolence is usually used with two meanings: without violence, or a struggle against violence. To state beforehand that an action is going to happen without violence can be important to give the police and participants a sense of security. Violence is here defined as any kind of action that can cause psychological or physical damage, including actions that create a panic situation. Police can, for example, become provoked if people run or yell slogans.

We human beings are imperfect and it is impossible to be completely free from violence. In connection with civil disobedience, for instance, we need to use cars or trains for transportation. By doing so, we support companies that participate in the arms trade, thereby contributing to the oppression of the Third World. Because of this it is more meaningful to use nonviolence in the sense of struggle against violence. Resistance is then always on two fronts. It is a political struggle against injustice in the society as well as a struggle with the violence inside ourselves. This acknowledgment of the latter aspect is due to feminist criticism of the nonviolence tradition during the 1970s. The women's movement viewed resistance as a mutual, collective struggle that was also within every resistance group. This is more fruitful than to advocate self-purification before every action, as Martin Luther King did. The purification enthusiasts create a spiritual hierarchy that excludes those of us that do not feel especially purified in our souls. Resistance demands instead that one is involved in situations that will make us feel desperate and afraid, or irritated and generally in a bad mood. It is probably more justified to say that resistance is preceded by a stomachache than purity.

Why Nonviolence?

There are two main arguments for nonviolence. One is practical and the other is ethical. The North American resistance expert Gene Sharp states simply that nonviolence is more effective than violence.[9] Violence leads to more violence while nonviolence counteracts it. Of course the resistance movement will suffer losses, even human lives, but the losses would be much greater if violence were used. A variation on this point of view is to claim that nonviolence is the only effective form of struggle today in *our* society. Those that claim this may accept violence on the part of guerrillas in *other places*, or military violence *later on* when a "foreign invader" attacks us.

Others advocate nonviolence from an ethical point of view. If one assumes that each person has an infinite value, then it follows that one person has as great a value as two or a thousand people. Many maintain the opposite: that two people have a greater value than one, and that one person could perhaps be sacrificed to save two. Their assumption must be that a human being's value is limited and not infinite, though it is always assumed to be extremely high. However, by restricting the value of a human being, they can justify sacrificing someone for the sake of the society.

No matter if one argues practically or ethically, nonviolence is a condition of civil disobedience. Since the actions and the consequences of the actions should be a moral challenge, a certain trust must be built up. This trust is impossible if the resistance group sometimes threatens to use violence; fear would create a mental block in people and make them unreceptive to the challenge. Civil disobedience becomes then a new breeding ground for fear. Disobedience in combination with violence strengthens the opponent's power. When social defense experts claim that it is possible to combine civil resistance with violent resistance, they have totally misunderstood the point of a resistance campaign. It is simply impossible to offer a police officer a cup of coffee at an action, if the cookies were poisoned at the last one.

CHAPTER II

COMMUNITY OF RESISTANCE:
ABOUT PREPARATIONS

CONFLICT AND COOPERATION

Preparation for civil disobedience consists above all in establishing an affinity group, preparing the action itself, and doing research. On the one hand, to establish an affinity group means breaking political isolation. However, it also means bringing conflicts out into the open and confronting the group with them. Community and conflict are both conditions of resistance.

Power and violence are historical phenomena. Specific examples of power and violence, like governments, the military, and prisons, have existed only during specific historical periods. We often view these things as self-evident; however, epochs have existed without wars or human cages. Other kinds of oppression can of course arise instead.

There has probably never been a time of such change as the epoch of capitalism. The increasing concentration of power and the extreme development of military violence make earlier empires pale by comparison. Due in part to the new world market, pretty much the whole world is now involved in all the wars. This can be hard to accept for all of us goodwilled reformists that live in a relatively peaceful part of the world; however, the situation also provides us with certain possibilities.

In spite of the rapid changes that have taken place during the last two hundred years, many people seem to think that things will remain the way they are now. This ahistorical perspective is, however, nothing new. For example, the emperor thought his empire would last forever, the slave owner considered slavery natural, and today's stock owner believes that people have always tried to make profits.

If we have a historical perspective, we try to understand each epoch and each culture according to its own special conditions. Whereas when we see the world from an ahistorical perspective, we explain, for example, the development of resistance all over the world according to the same conditions. These two perspectives can stimulate each other.

An ahistorical comparison between different cultures allows the discovery of similarities that are not completely culturally determined. Perhaps these similarities indicate that we have basic needs of cooperation and affinity that cause certain ethical principles to arise in historical situations that are totally different from each other. Yet research about nonviolence is often ahistorical in a negative sense. North American resistance expert Gene Sharp, for example, has counted 198 different types of nonviolent actions.[10] Now he is supposed to have an even longer list. This classification is certainly interesting as an inspiring list of ideas. However, a form of resistance can mean one thing in one society and something completely different in another. It is not so easy to compare, for example, the independence movement in India with our own struggle for solidarity with the Third World. Gandhi's experiences in India must be seen as a national struggle for independence from a colonial power, while the struggle in many parts of Latin America is rather a struggle for freedom from economic and political conditions.

How can we in Western democracies understand our own resistance? When I taught a course in civil disobedience in Chile during the spring of 1988, I had the opportunity, together with the participants, of clarifying some of the significant differences between civil disobedience in a democracy and civil disobedience under a dictatorship. After a while we nevertheless started to find basic similarities. Economically speaking, both the participants and I lived in liberal societies. This meant that we theoretically had a large number of possibilities as far as choosing education, a home, and our place of work. Since there is a limited number of choices and a lack of institutions for mediation that can facilitate common solutions, we have to compete with others that want the same thing. This competition creates a society where citizens perceive themselves more as individuals than as a part of a group.

The social Darwinists and the early liberals maintained that competition steered the development of society. Karl Marx maintained instead that it is the struggle of the classes with each other that creates history. The Russian anarchist and prince Petr Kropotkin tried instead to define mutual aid as the driving force of history, using examples from nature to prove his theory.[11] These classic theories provide an important insight: changes arise through either cooperation or conflict.

Both cooperation and conflict can happen on different levels: within groups, between individuals or between an individual and a group. Conflicts even arise within the individual. It is from this perspective that Phil Berrigan, one of the founders of the Plowshares movement, asserts that resistance arises from community.[12] This mutual, creative process is not a purely harmonious state; it means both cooperation and conflict. This idea helps us understand the very need for resistance. When conflicts arise in this mutually creative process, negotiations are needed that will lead to agreement and a new creative process. When these negotiations are stalled and one party's opinions are ignored, resistance is necessary to get the dialogue going again.

Cooperation between different groups in society is a prerequisite in the struggle against powerful opponents. Gandhi furthered this point in an interesting way: the struggle additionally demanded supporting the opponents when they had problems. This support could then lead to cooperation with the opponent, even while the resistance is in progress. Consequently, we support representatives of the opposing party that support the resistance movement. Daniel Ellsberg, who worked as a U.S. presidential adviser during the 1960s, published the top secret "Pentagon Papers" during the Vietnam War. These papers revealed the brutal tactics used in Vietnam by the U.S. When he was indicted, the peace movement gave him strong support. Twenty years later, he is helping the Plowshares movement, acting as a witness at trials. The Plowshares movement has also been helped by an ex-attorney general, Ramsey Clark. This cooperation has led to several judges' direct participation in civil disobedience.

However, community is not just cooperation, but also conflict. A sense of community can be experienced as threatening. If we don't allow each other to be different, then a sense of community can become a prison, resulting in isolation. This does not necessarily mean isolation in an emotional or private sense, but isolation in a political sense. We do not turn to each other to solve common problems. The different collective movements' struggle for my interests is perceived neither as *my* struggle nor as *our* struggle, but as *their* struggle. Overcoming this political isolation is the first goal of resistance.

Inside the peace and solidarity movements people have sometimes become so enthusiastic about openings in communication that they have chosen to suppress existing conflicts. This is dangerous. Those who adapt their statements to the opponent's opinions create a *false consensus* where everybody seems to agree. But people see through such things and their sense of commitment is reduced. To achieve cooperation we must be aware of conflicts. If we want to establish an agreement, we must look at the disagreements. Otherwise, we end up in the strange situation that has arisen many times before: protesting groups are so moderate in their recommendations that they are quickly surpassed by the politicians that they have been criticizing.

Obedience and Fear

What is needed to stop a company that destroys the environment or exports arms?

When I ask this of participants in my courses, they usually stare at me, confused. But within a few minutes they have a plan ready. Not many disobedient telephone workers, postal workers, transport workers, or bank workers are needed to stop a certain activity. The more complex our society becomes, the greater the dependence on cooperation at all possible levels. This dependence is increasing more and more for both governments and companies as the economy becomes more and more international. This therefore is an ideal development for those of us that use civil disobedience. However, it is not that simple. The problem is that in reality we obey. Obedience is rooted somewhere deep within us.

The sociologist Max Weber points out that we often submit voluntarily to authority. Those in power are perceived as legitimate authorities. Our support of them can be based on the leaders' charisma and our own devotion. Obedience can also arise from our belief in the inviolability of tradition. We think: "That is the way it is and therefore it must be right." Of course, obedience can also be based on a sensible way of reasoning: "Things are OK the way they are and I don't want to risk a change for the worse...."

There are, however, large groups that think that many of the decisions made by the authorities or companies are not legitimate. It is surprising that whether we call ourselves pacifists, revolutionaries, reformists, socialists, syndicalists, anarchists, Marxists, liberals, environmentalists, feminists, or nonviolent activists—obedience still seems to be self-evident. Choose any one of these groups. This group in itself would be enough to stop most environmental destruction or arms exports if its members used civil disobedience. Often, a few people who regularly carry out actions to create strong moral pressure are enough to get negotiations going with the opponent. Examples include all the occupations to save houses and cultural landmarks that were common during the 1970s and 1980s in Europe. Phil Berrigan was imprisoned several times during the Vietnam War. According to him, at most a few hundred people were in prison for civil disobedience at this time. The actions of this relatively small group together with lawful demonstrations created heavy pressure on the government of the United States.

There is a special reason why the radical, socially aware people obey: we want to be able to calculate the personal consequences of our actions. We are simply afraid of the personal implications of disobedience. I mentioned earlier that overcoming political isolation was the first goal of the struggle. The second goal is overcoming fear of the consequences. That is what all nonviolence is about. Our enemy is not the government or the company bosses. Fear is the enemy. We can use civil disobedience to challenge each other to dismantle the walls of fear and thus to overcome obedience.

Affinity Groups

Gandhi said that nonviolent resistance was impossible without *fearlessness*. To be able to carry out resistance we must free ourselves from fear of risking our possessions, honor, family, and relatives, and from fear of the government, bodily injuries, and death. According to Gandhi, physical strength is not needed in order to do this. One person or a million people can offer resistance. Women and men alike can participate. The only thing needed is psychological self-control. This fearlessness, says Gandhi, can arise from a constant attempt to understand what truth and nonviolence are.[13]

Martin Luther King suggested, as I mentioned earlier, that civil disobedience should be preceded by self-cleansing. Both men's solutions for overcoming fear emphasize individual, spiritual preparation.

This tradition has developed in different directions. In religious groups, the concept of "civil disobedience of the spiritually strong" was used. Especially among young men, "professional resistance" developed. The idea here was that those who had been arrested several times knew what was going to happen and could carry out actions without very much preparation.

These approaches were criticized by some feminists and members of the Plowshares movement, who argued that it was too elitist and individualistic an approach to preparations for an action. This form of resistance became a struggle for the brave. The Plowshares movement is, to a certain extent, a reaction against this. It consists of people that seldom see themselves as especially brave or convinced. Mutual support has come widely to be seen as an alternative to individual spiritual strength. By creating trust in small groups, the fear of personal consequences can be overcome. Community becomes the foundation of resistance.

During a large action at the Seabrook nuclear power plant in New Hampshire in 1976, the idea of affinity groups was used for the first time since the Spanish Civil War. During the thirties, the anarchist movement in Spain had based their resistance activities partly on *grupos de affinidad*. The result of the renaissance of this idea surpassed all expectations, and it spread quickly all over the U.S. Through the growing international peace movement at the beginning of the eighties, the idea spread to the rest of the Western world. I make a sharp distinction between civil disobedience before and after Seabrook. Affinity groups have revolutionized nonviolent resistance! Before, one had to rely on strong, charismatic leaders or just hope that the action went all right. With affinity groups, all the members participate in planning, decisionmaking, and carrying out the decisions. Democracy in the nonviolent movement has taken a big step forward.

An affinity group is an action group that participates in civil disobedience. It usually is made up of three to fifteen people. It is often an advantage not to be too many. In my first affinity group, formed in 1982, we were three people. Affinity groups are formed before actions and can be dissolved when any resulting jail sentences have been served. There are also continuous affinity groups that participate in a longer action campaign and do civil disobedience regularly.

Affinity groups have several advantages over individual actions or the former type of mass action. The most important is that the level of democracy is increased. Affinity groups are self-governing and are responsible for the whole action. This makes participation something entirely different from when a group of leaders is involved. The first time I participated in an action with over one thousand people, all in affinity groups, I had not really understood the great difference in comparison with an action where just a few people controlled the course of events. Every participant had planned the blockade! Some people offered coffee to the police and military. Buddhist nuns and monks from Japan held drummed prayer meetings succeeded by Catholic masses. A women's affinity group blocked the military's landing strip. Others planted trees. This kind of creativity, due to the presence of affinity groups, obviously makes the quality of an action much higher.

Another advantage is that decisionmaking often goes faster in an affinity group. The members can quickly be collected when new, unexpected situations arise. Furthermore, the continuity of resistance is increased with affinity groups, since many choose to continue to work together and do new actions. After our big blockade, many affinity groups wanted to continue. Organized into affinity groups, one thousand people also have more energy to escalate the resistance than a small group of leaders who burn out quickly. We organized a ten-day campaign with actions every day. One or two affinity groups were responsible for each day. My affinity group organized a Greek folk dance on the airport's landing strip.

Affinity groups also guarantee that the experience of planning actions is shared. Otherwise the risk increases that a movement can be weakened if its leaders are weakened. A clear example of this was when several civil rights groups more or less disappeared after Martin Luther King was shot.

Another advantage of affinity groups is that they reduce the possibilities for provocateurs to infiltrate, at least if every participant in an action is required to belong to an affinity group. Members of an affinity group know each other very well, and it is not unusual that someone who does not accept the guidelines of nonviolence is asked to leave the group. If someone should in spite of everything lose control at an action, his or her affinity group is immediately at hand to give support. Posting a requirement that all participants should belong to an affinity group increases the sense of security for both the participants and police. Every affinity group reports in advance what they plan to do. The risk of provocation is thereby minimized.

One disadvantage with affinity groups can be that it becomes more difficult to participate in occasional civil disobedience. Affinity groups create a sense of commitment that also demands a lot of time.

Responsibilities in an Affinity Group

In an affinity group, responsibility is divided up between the participants. Half of the group usually expects to get arrested, and the rest are support people. Surprisingly, the support people are the most active during the action. Before doing civil disobedience myself, I had expected just the opposite.

The support people can be divided into peacekeepers, contact people, and those "personal supporters" that help the activists with practical things. None of these duties usually leads to arrest. **Peacekeepers** are responsible for maintaining the peace during an action. Special training in peacekeeping is held that includes such things as how to handle provocative people and how to calm down upset spectators. The peacekeepers in the Livermore Action Group in California had armbands on during actions. They informed the police which people were peacekeepers and the police avoided arresting them. The idea of armbands is debatable, however. Some people think that special symbols for peacekeepers are too much like uniforms. At big actions, peacekeepers from different affinity groups divide up the responsibilities among them. Some have the job of keeping the police calm and others calm the spectators or workers.

Some are responsible for seeing that the activists themselves do not act in a provocative manner.

Usually peacekeepers try to create some kind of personal contact with each member of the police before he or she arrests an activist. Even the workers involved are usually contacted, though it is best to do this before the action begins. The purpose of this kind of personal contact is, of course, to help the opponent understand the action. In addition, it becomes more difficult for opponents to use brutal violence against people with whom they have had a calm, normal contact. The fact that peacekeepers and activists, in this case, don't happen to be the same people doesn't seem to be of any importance.

In the spring of 1988, I was a spectator in Chile at an action against torture. Suddenly a police bus started to drive over the sitting activists. The activists had trouble establishing contact with the driver until one of the support people spontaneously took on the role of peacekeeper. He started talking with the driver through the side window. This direct address caused the driver to relax and back the bus away.

A peacekeeper must be prepared for completely unexpected situations. In 1983, I was a peacekeeper at an action at the arms factory Bofors Aerotronics on an island near Stockholm. A Lutheran minister, Eva Brunne, was holding a memorial service for people who had been killed by Swedish weapons. After a while some teenagers started shouting. I responded by asking to interview them. Without saying what I thought myself, I got them to reflect on themselves and the action by asking numerous questions. After the interview we received support from them instead.

The **contact people** function as another important support. They coordinate among different affinity groups, call up the families and friends of the activists who have been arrested, make contact with lawyers, prosecuting attorneys and judges, mediate with the police, function as spokespersons by giving interviews for the media, and contact other organizations for support statements. Most contact people are on the scene of the action while others remain somewhere near a telephone or fax machine.

Personal supporters have central tasks in an affinity group. They give direct support to those that risk being arrested. Their responsibilities include making sure extra clothing, medicine, and food is available, and collecting what has been left behind after the arrests have been made. They also follow the police cars and wait outside the police station to be on hand to receive arrested activists if they are released. Remember that arrested people are not always taken to the nearest police station, nor to the one the police used last time.

Some of my friends were arrested at a big action in Germany. Together with several hundred other activists, they were driven to the next city over and released. In this way, the police wanted to prevent the activists from returning to the action. But the support people showed foresight and followed the convoy of prisoners. They were able to convey the activists back to the action as soon as they were released.

PREPARATIONS FOR AN ACTION

At my first Plowshares meeting, we met in an old, run-down church in a Black ghetto in New York City. Earlier, I had met several Plowshares activists at a party after the disarmament of a B-52 bomber. None of those for whom we were celebrating were actually there: they were behind bars at a police station nearby. But many of the people active in the Plowshares movement were there. The party was a lot of fun.

It was packed with people and I had to squeeze my way into a place on the floor. I found myself in the middle of a discussion about all the mistakes and weaknesses of the Plowshares movement. I knew almost nothing about the movement, but I managed to pick up a little during the discussion.

After the party I lay awake all night. Finally I made up my mind. I contacted one of the people that had been most critical during the discussion. She had helped with coordination of the research and other preparations before the disarmament of the airplane. I asked her if they would have any use of a Swede in the next group. A couple of months later I was invited to New York City.

When I first came in contact with them, I associated the Plowshares movement with the disarmament of weapons and the many years of imprisonment that was sometimes the result of their actions. I now think, however, that their most important contribution is the way in which the groups prepare themselves for an action. Because of this, I will use different Plowshares groups' preparations as examples of how to prepare an action. I think their experiences are of interest for solidarity and environmental actions as well.

A Plowshares action is not just the disarmament of weapons:

- In our discussions we try to disarm our own fears as well.
- We also disarm other kinds of protection that we have built up to avoid taking personal risks.
- We even try to disarm the violence and oppression that exists within the group.
- Finally, through the action, we start disarming the society from violence, fear, and suspicion.

This disarmament is not about personal development, nor is it a way to gain peace of mind. The result is in fact instead sometimes chaotic. We try to overcome fear not in order to get rid of it, but to give us the courage to do civil disobedience. The fear is still there. We don't do resistance against oppression within the group so that conflicts will disappear. But these conflicts do have to be dealt with so that democracy can function.

This method's roots can be traced to Catholic monasteries. In the middle of the 1960s, nuns, Jesuits, and Trappist monks took the radical step from protest to resistance against the Vietnam War. They continued to prepare themselves as they had always done before going out to work in the world. This tradition developed over time. During the 1970s the Atlantic Life Community was created as a network of resistance groups. The Plowshares movement was born from this network in 1980. The movement is the grandchild of the meeting between Catholic piety and radical groups in the 1960s.

Since the Plowshares movement was inspired by some aspects of the Christian tradition, many people think that it is also specifically Christian. This is incorrect. In my first group—Pershing Plowshares—there was a practicing Jew and a Buddhist. In other groups in which I have been a support person, atheists, agnostics, and pagans have participated. The movement has a broad political base as well, with both liberals and leftists participating in Plowshares actions.

Every Plowshares group is independent and develops its own experiences and ideas. There is, however, a tradition that has been created within the Atlantic Life Community, which many Plowshares groups continue to develop. This experience can be of help to new groups. But a tradition should not be perceived as a demand; every Plowshares group breaks some part of the tradition.

The goal of a Plowshares group is usually to create a resistance community. The method used to achieve this is reflection and discussion of texts. These texts consist of novels and poetry as well as more theoretical works. For example, if we discuss a certain law, the person who has prepared this point on the agenda reads a text that deals with an aspect of what the law means. Usually we reflect for a moment in silence about the text. Then each person shares his or her thoughts with the others. After everyone has spoken, the discussion begins. The preeminent question is: what relevance does the text have for us and for society? We call this interpreting or reinterpreting the text. However, it is just as important to criticize the text and to confront different experiences and texts with each other.

The groups I have participated in usually met for three days at a time. During such a **retreat** we often have time to discuss up to six or seven subjects. Before the group feels ready to do an action, it can be necessary to have between five and ten retreats. In Sweden, we have had a few really long preparations for actions. In the United States and Germany, the groups have prepared themselves somewhat faster. In the Netherlands, I don't think the first group prepared itself at all. They did four disarmament actions in a row and taunted us Germans and Swedes, saying that we talked too much.

Instead of spending a lot of time on detail-planning and meetings, most Plowshares groups choose to have retreats. A retreat provides the opportunity to take a break from doing, and instead reflect over what has to be done. For a resistance group, this means using a holistic approach based on personal needs, the group's needs, and the society's needs. We combine a form of individualism with strong collectivism. These preparations usually have three functions:

- To create a resistance community and to challenge this community.
- To develop the nonviolent tradition.
- To plan a Plowshares action.

These three things are developed simultaneously during the preparation retreats and are, of course, impossible to completely separate from each other.

Creating a resistance community consists partly of getting to know each other and developing a functional cooperation. We do this by continuously evaluating and questioning our cooperation. Before an action, we also question each individual's ability to carry it out. Each activist is given the opportunity to consider the hesitations that the others might have about his or her participation. In most groups, at least a few of the participants realize that they should probably wait a while before doing an action.

Conflicts always occur in intensive groups like these. Using different methods, these conflicts can be identified and attempts can be made to solve them. Through conflicts a feeling of community can be developed. However, in order for the group to function there must be support and a sense of security within the group. A feeling of mutual trust is necessary in order to give and receive criticism in a constructive way. In fact, without this mutual support it is difficult to get a critical discussion going at all. Critical discussions are crucial in stimulating the development of a strong resistance based on experience and reflection.

Our discussions and analyses can be about law, the current political situation, militarism, the media, the resistance movement, the alternative movement in general, political parties, feminism, racism, democracy, violence, nonviolence, civil disobedience, destruction of property, oppression, dominance, oppression within the group, and more. We also try to approach philosophical problems, such as: How are ethics established? What right do we have to break the law? What kind of moral consequences does our profession of nonviolence have? Each question can take one to several hours to discuss. Each discussion is both a reflection on a text and the beneficiary of earlier discussions.

These preparations are therefore an ongoing distillation of the experiences of the group into new thoughts. Every Plowshares group also does research that is of importance for the resistance movement as a whole. This is in accordance with Gandhi's goals for the actions that he participated in.[14] All this taken together means that the Plowshares process probably provides one of the most profound educations in civil disobedience available at the moment.

During the whole process, we alternate these political and philosophical discussions with conversations about fear and risks, security, support and loneliness, arrest and detention, trial and punishment, ours and others' safety, family and friends, and more. Even if we don't spend much time planning all the details of an action, we do discuss the action's message, motive, symbols, and priorities. We talk about something called the action's focus. This means concentration on what is most important, and deciding means that are strong enough, instead of using our limited resources for all kinds of issues and actions. Focus also means clarity. Is the action understandable? Is the message really a challenge? To whom is the action directed and how can this target group be reached?

We also discuss possible ways of achieving change. Which media can we use to create a dialogue with the opponent and the rest of society? What actually communicates the message? Some communication forms include trials, personal contact with workers and decisionmakers, letters, courses, and seminars. Perhaps the most important vehicle for disarmament is starting new Plowshares groups. A critical concern of the movement is to place the responsibility for disarmament of weapons on the citizens of a society, not the official decisionmakers.

Alongside retreats we do research, which usually means making countless telephone calls and going through innumerable documents. We also visit factories and military bases and investigate the group's possibilities of carrying out an action. A few days before the action, we role-play different situations, like interrogation or the guards' discovery of the action. By trying to imagine what might happen, we can avoid situations and behavior that are provocative.

Of course, retreats are not always as serious as my description might make them sound. Parties, games, ceremonies, dances, and songs are just as important as the discussions. But nobody needs a handbook on how to have parties, so I leave that up to the reader's own creativity.

Research

When we do research for a Plowshares action, we usually use official sources of information. Surprisingly, we have obtained quite a lot of information from visits, annual reports, applications to the government made by companies, drawings, and maps. To gain information about ownership and profits, we contact the library and different public authorities. The telephone book is invaluable. Aside from providing information about the positions and departments within a company, as well as its address, it enables you to just call and ask for the information you need. Receptionists are usually very service-oriented!

When we investigate a public authority, we call or write to the department that we are interested in and order what we need. During visits you can ask to see daily logs of letters, faxes, and other documents. These logs contain short summaries of the documents. A couple of my friends visited the Swedish security police. By reading the daily logs, they found out that the Immigration Board regularly asked for information from the security police about certain refugees.

Based on information in the daily logs, they asked for both secret and official documents. If they didn't get the documents they wanted, they appealed the decision. In several countries, the authorities have to reassess the secret classification of a document every time it is requested by someone. By asking officials carefully prepared questions, you can get a lot of information. If you really want to get what you are looking for, you will probably have to make several visits.

Some groups only work on keeping corporations and public authorities under surveillance. These are sometimes called "Little Sisters." Big Brother in effect just has to accept that he is also being watched. Highlighting this aspect, in Norway one group is called "Little Brother." When I lived in the U.S., I read a newspaper published by an equivalent organization, whose only activity was to watch the controlling bodies of the public authorities.

To facilitate alternative political information exchange, different databases around the world have been consolidated. The first such computer networks were PeaceNet in the United States and GreenNet in England. These are now connected to an international network, which is called the Association for Progressive Communication. Groups in the Nordic countries and even groups in Russia, Australia, Brazil, and Canada are connecting their databases to this network. I bought a modem that allowed me to connect my computer to the telephone. I could then access or add information to this network. When I needed information for this handbook, I sometimes posted a question on the network and received answers a few days later.

Sometimes official channels are insufficient. In order to find a good place to do an action you must visit the proposed site beforehand. Once there, you should examine storage areas, locks, and fences, and notice the different areas as well as the routines of the guards. Both for the planning and for the trial it can be useful to make a map of the area.

We hardly ever know where to start our research. Each time we have clumsily improvised at the beginning. But after a while, the right context becomes more clear. In one case, a Swedish-Norwegian group that was considering doing a Plowshares action tried to find out if nuclear-armed airplanes landed at Rygge military air base, outside of Oslo. Another activist, Henrik Frykberg, and I offered to watch the airstrip from inside the base for three days. After being followed and stopped twice, we finally found a good place on a field. Though we didn't know what airplanes carrying nuclear weapons looked like, we had Jane's *All the World's Aircraft* with us.[15] During the first few hours we just stared at the planes as they landed and took off again. After a while, we learned how to identify certain distinctive features. Henrik became experienced at quickly raising his binoculars so that he could see the country designations of the planes. I had to quickly flip through the handbook and try to recognize any protruding tailfins or backwards-bent wings. This was enough for two amateurs to be able to find out if airplanes with nuclear weapons capacity land at a military airport.

In another case, two members of Swedish Plowshares, Gunilla Åkerberg and Anders Grip, planned to disarm a Bofors cannon that was to be transported by train. However, they did not know which route the train was supposed to take. Quite quickly, however, they found out the usual routines with such transports. People who lived along the railroad tracks could tell them when the train passed and when the switch-tenders worked. Even more important, they knew when the tracks were not switched. It became apparent that the trains hardly had any realistic alternative routes. In addition, the cannons were too big to be effectively transported along the regular highways. After a while, only a few possibilities remained and these were covered by support people who took walks along the railroad tracks.

After a week, on Thursday, one of the harbor workers called and told them that the cannons had been loaded. The Plowshares group's morale hit bottom. Many weeks of tension and stressful waiting had come to nothing. Everybody wanted to go home. One of the support people offered to go and take a last look before the group broke up. Feeling dejected, he walked over to the train station to buy candy at the shop there. After he paid he turned around and there were five Bofors cannons, Fälthaubits 77Bs, each one on its own railcar. He just stared at them in amazement. Then he ran all the way back to the group. Breathlessly, he told them what he had seen, but of course nobody believed him. When he finally succeeded in convincing them, the group took a moment just to calm down. Then they got into Gunilla's old Volvo and drove to the station. After getting lost once, they managed to find the area where the track switches were, next to the train station. Without anybody there to stop them, they then proceeded to do the first Swedish disarmament action.

SECURITY AND INFILTRATION

An effective way of paralyzing a group is to spread the rumor that they are being bugged or infiltrated. Even more effective is to see to it that an infiltrator or a microphone is actually exposed. In his book *Spy Catcher*, Peter Wright describes a similar tactic used effectively by the former Soviet Union to paralyze Western intelligence agencies during the 1950s.[16] They sent dissidents over to disclose how widespread infiltration of the Western world's security system was. Even

Wright, who at the time worked for the British military counterintelligence, MI 5, which functions as the British security agency, believed these rumors at first. The FBI developed this tactic and used it effectively during the sixties and seventies, succeeding in making leftist groups more sectarian. The sheer numbers of infiltrators exposed within different U.S. groups shows that the police were not especially concerned about keeping attempts at infiltration secret.

The same methods have been used against the contemporary alternative movement. Orlando's Freeze, a group in Florida that functioned as our support group at the Plowshares action in 1984, was subjected to at least three infiltrators. Bruce Gagnon, a member of the group who exposed two of the infiltrators, wrote an open letter to the police asking them to call instead when they wanted to know something. A peace group in Syracuse, New York, where I volunteered for a year was able to gain access to large sections of the FBI's file on them while Jimmy Carter was president. Reagan later stopped this access to information. The FBI file on them was at least two inches thick. Now and then the FBI had sent in infiltrators. Some of my friends told me that they were able to point out several of them.

This is where the real problem is. The feeling of suspicion caused everybody to brand people who acted a little strange as infiltrators. Several of us realized that the only solution was to keep acting out in the open. If we became uncertain as to how much the police knew, we just sent a letter directly to them. Then there was no longer any doubt! Others thought that we should act more "professionally," i.e., we should be more careful about what we said and who we said it to.

These two attitudes lead to two completely different movements. Openness is a condition for democracy. To be able to make sensible decisions you need to have access to all the relevant, available information. A managerial top stratum that has access to more information than the others functions more like a system with an enlightened despot than a democracy. A secret organization has trouble maintaining its democratic dynamics, and it also becomes difficult for the group to gain wide support. It is therefore important to resist attempts to make an organization more sectarian and secret. Suspicion helps only those who want to control the movement. On the other hand, I do not want to imply that those who want more "professionalism" or "secretiveness" are infiltrators.

Since civil disobedience is founded on openness, I will not go into how to protect a group from surveillance. Openness can neutralize attempts to manipulate and to provoke a resistance group. Of course, it is important to keep refugees' hiding places a secret. During short periods of time, it might be necessary to keep certain things secret, such as before an action. Continuously working in secret, however, creates strange dynamics after a while.

There is a difference between security and intelligence, each of which can be private or state-run. Usually the Department of State, the police, and the military are in charge of the state-run services. A security service is responsible for protecting its employer. The private security sector has expanded dramatically during the eighties. According to recent articles in two Swedish newspapers, the private security sector has more employees than the police.[17] Large organizations like the Catholic Church or unions can have their own security services.

The military or police security service should, according to tradition, work with counterintelligence and make sure that the state is not threatened in any way. The state is seldom threatened by common criminality, so security services mainly watch political activities. The security police of Sweden, Säpo, keeps both the environmental and the peace movements under surveillance. When this was exposed, the chief of the security police, Mats Börjesson, pointed out that both movements ought to be grateful that they were under surveillance. He was of the opinion that they needed Säpo to protect them from communist infiltration.[18]

Any intelligence service worth its name spies. Practically speaking, it is difficult to differentiate between a security agency and an intelligence agency. It is also difficult to identify their areas of responsibility. Philip Agee, a CIA agent who quit, states in his journal that the CIA has three main duties: to manipulate and infiltrate, to spread disinformation, and to spy.[19] According to Agee, infiltration was successfully aimed at political parties, youth organizations, labor unions, state agencies, and similar targets. The purpose was to control these organizations, which was made relatively easy because most of them had a similar hierarchical structure. The aim can, of course, also have been simply to gather information.

An expensive way to infiltrate is to use one's own personnel. More commonly, however, ignored, dissatisfied people waltz into the United States' embassies and offer their services. According to Agee, it isn't especially difficult to find people with wavering loyalty, even in labor unions and leftist political parties. When our support group, the local Freeze group in Orlando, was infiltrated, actual police were used twice. However, in one case they used a person that was accused of a crime and hoped to escape punishment by doing the police a service.

The second main area of the CIA's activity is disinformation. If you read the daily papers carefully, you find now and then articles that must be the result of the CIA's or some similar agency's propaganda machinery. A relatively obvious example is how information about injustices done by countries or organizations that are against the United States reaches the mass media with unbelievable speed. In the former socialist countries, people developed an ability to read between the lines and see through the massive state propaganda machinery.

Agee divides propaganda into three categories. White propaganda is official. Gray propaganda is spread via organizations and individuals that seem to be independent. Black propaganda is anonymous or comes from false sources.[20] Disinformation can be both lies and half-truths. The aim of disinformation is to control a course of events. Sometimes direct and obvious, usually, however, this control is more sophisticated and indirect. The Swedish security police have, for example, "accidentally" leaked a list of the parliamentarians that have visited prostitutes. This is a clear reminder to all politicians and higher officials: if they are involved in activities that they don't want to become public, then they had better do what the security police wants. The journalists and newspapers that use disinformation are usually not aware of the purposes behind it.

People who criticize the security agencies risk being defamed or having their secrets exposed. At least three high officials in Sweden have been subjected to leaks from the security police. All three worked for the Department of State, were in some way critical of the security police, and tried to change its way of working.

Even movements that are critical of the society can be the objects of similar smear campaigns. For example, fanatic religious groups can spread pamphlets that state that the peace movement uses devil symbols. A schism between the peace movement and Christian churches might be created in this way. A radical cooperation would be catastrophic for the military, since Christian churches probably have the largest number of active members of any movement in the rich world. A smear campaign designed to achieve quick results is usually most effective if directed at the leaders of a movement. Several so-called scandals concerning Mahatma Gandhi's and Martin Luther King's private lives were spread by state propaganda agencies.[21]

Provocation can also function as disinformation. Gunnar Ekberg worked for the Swedish military intelligence. He infiltrated several Swedish Vietnam and Palestine groups at the end of the sixties and beginning of the seventies. By, among other things, sneaking anti-Semitic propaganda into their flyers, he managed to defame the Palestine movement. But he was above all a spy.[22]

The informer is an important source of more complete information. When I studied Spanish at a university in Ecuador, I met Swedish missionaries who had studied Spanish at a missionary school in Costa Rica. They told me that the CIA recruited informers among the North American students at the missionary school. The Swedish missionaries could guess which of their classmates were recruited. One simple method of finding out was to ask if anyone had tried to recruit them. If the answer was affirmative but that they had said no, then that was probably the truth. If, on the other hand, the person questioned didn't want to talk about it, then they might have been recruited.

Espionage is a huge, bureaucratic business today. Mainly it consists of analyzing information from newspapers or other official sources. There are also well-developed technical investigation operations carried out with the help of radar and interception of communications via radio waves. Radio communications are recorded and saved until somebody leaks the code or the intelligence agency breaks it.

It is likely that a small intelligence service gets most of its information from official sources and exchanges with other espionage organizations. Exchanges usually consist of routine sending back and forth of analyses and information. It is assumed that the favor will be returned by providing similar information and showing a certain amount of loyalty. Important, specific information can, however, be "sold" or exchanged for certain favors as on a market.

If a security agency wants to be a credible collaborator, then it might have to provide information about refugee organizations, political parties, labor unions, and protest movements. A small country pretty quickly finds itself in a state of dependence when it cooperates with one of the superpowers' intelligence services. The Swedish security police have even stated that it would paralyze vital areas of their activities if the CIA stopped giving them information. This happened after the Swedish government officially protested on February 23, 1979 against the fact that the FBI had used a high Swedish police official for espionage on, among others, Iraqi citizens. This protest had to be quieted down so that Sweden's relationship with the CIA could improve again.[23]

Surveillance

The strength of nonviolence comes from not playing according to the opponent's rules. To indicate just how difficult it would be to start playing the same games as the privately or publicly employed spies, I will describe how professional hide-and-seek is played. William J. Davis is a priest who investigates private and state espionage of churches and solidarity groups in the United States. He has shown, for example, how recent technological developments here made bugging a simple, routine job.[24] By using techniques similar to the telephone company's answering service, telephones all over the country, including pay phones, can be quickly bugged.

With the help of certain trigger words like "resistance" or "Central America," computers can save and sort recordings or erase them if they are uninteresting. It is now possible to bug all of the members of a labor union even if it has several hundred thousand members. Most recordings made during mass bugging with the help of computerized key words are, of course, erased after a certain period of time. Only those that the computer considers interesting are saved and actually listened to.

Older telephones' metal bells can be activated with a sensitive amplifier and a filter as a bugging device even when the receiver is hung up. The person who wants to bug a certain telephone number calls that number. When the receiver is picked up the bugging begins. It is then possible to continue to listen to what is said in the room even after the owner of the telephone hangs up. Peter Wright describes another way of transforming a regular telephone into a bugging device. If a strong radio signal is directed from a relatively short distance toward a telephone receiver, then the receiver is activated as a bugging device. When a worker from the telephone company installed a telephone for me once, he showed me one of his standard instruments. It registered the currents in the telephone wires. These weak currents were amplified and provided enough power to run a small speaker. When he held the instrument close to a wall, we could hear not only where the telephone wires were, but also what was said. Anybody could use an instrument like that. For the more professional type, there is the option of sending the signals on into the telephone network and then to a tape recorder.

A simpler way to send signals is with a little radio transmitter. One of the more common kinds, easily built at home, transmits on 103 megahertz. The Employers Confederation transmits its local radio propaganda in my home town on nearly the same frequency, which has caused irritation for those bugging and merriment for those being bugged. Bugging devices can also intercept vibrations of your voice from furniture or windows. This can be done with a laser, for instance, or by putting a sensitive microphone against the vibrating surface. People who sought out dissidents in socialist dictatorships a few years ago witnessed them turning up the radio and directing the speakers toward the windows and the ceiling. Then they would whisper. Other dissidents spoke out more publicly. They wanted instead to get people used to speaking freely without fear.

One way of finding out if someone is bugging you is to put the telephone receiver close to your grandmother's tube radio. Turn the frequency dial until you hear Jimi Hendrix's screaming guitar. The bug is then sending on the same frequency as the one the radio is tuned to; the phone feeds back the signal from the radio. Please, tell the man sitting in a cellar somewhere to take off his headphones before you try this.

Aside from bugging, an active surveillance can mean that a person's mail is opened. A friend of mine in the United States never got mail on Saturday, which was strange since all of her neighbors received mail then. Not only that, she was an activist and got an unusually large amount of mail. She helped the Plowshares movement investigate military bases and helped refugees go into hiding. She suspected that her mail was gone through on a regular basis. She lived in a small town and there wasn't much activity at the local police station on the weekends. My friend had to wait patiently until the weekend mail could be gone through on Monday. The connection was so clear that it seemed that the letter openers wanted her to know that she was being watched. It was a way of keeping her under control more than of getting information.

Envelopes can be opened with the help of a steaming coffeepot. If the envelope is taped shut then you have to find a small opening, according to Peter Wright. A split bamboo stick is poked in. If the letter paper is in the opening it can be rolled up and drawn out. If that is impossible, the envelope can be ripped open and a copy made of it later.

Traditional shadowing can be exposed through different traps. The easiest way is to go down a dead-end street and simply turn around. Another way is to place friends along your route. When you suddenly go in another direction or turn around, your friends can perhaps discover the person who is tailing you. In this way, the former Soviet Union's embassy was able to keep tabs on the people who kept their employees under surveillance during the forties and fifties. Peter Wright talks about situations where it was important that the tailing was not exposed. Then they only allowed their agents to follow the victim for a very short time. If the victim turned off, then they were not followed. In this way they avoided making quick, amateurish jumps into doorways when the victim turned around. With the help of a communications system and a map, they could tell another agent to take over on the next street. William J. Davis mentions the possibility of following the tracks of the person being tailed with a specially built camera. It is also possible to put a radio transmitter on the victim. Then the tailers can go home and play dominoes while the bus trip or mountain hike is registered on a map.

Davis claims that cars used for tailing can even have changeover switches for their headlights. When the tailed car turns off onto another road, the car following behind switches its headlights so it seems like there is a different car behind. A more realistic alternative is to use several cars that relieve each other. When the car that is being tailed turns off, a car that is further back takes over.

Active surveillance is expensive. The nonviolence movement is probably not under surveillance to any great extent. When it is discovered that the movement is being watched, the intent can just as well be to cause us to become more suspicious toward each other as to gain information. An employee of Bofors, a Swedish weapons manufacturer, was told by the security department of the company that all the members of a Plowshares group were registered, even the support people. How had they found out which people were involved? It is just as important to ask how we found out about the register. Was the leak intentional? Was it only disinformation to make us paranoid?

I usually take it for granted that Big Brother can see everything. He is probably not especially interested. But as long as I am not afraid of his knowledge then it is not a threat to my work.

"But!" objects the pensive reader. "How are we to hide refugees or do a surprise action?"

One has to differentiate between the local police, the Immigration and Naturalization Service, and the security agencies. A security agency hardly has any reason to stop an act of civil disobedience; they would only expose themselves. Exposure can also be politically sensitive if it is made public. The ordinary police, on the other hand, seldom have the resources or permission necessary to watch the alternative or solidarity movements.

What are the limits of openness? As far as investigations or surprise actions go, a certain cautiousness can be justified. You should not say the name of a refugee's hiding place on the phone. Since the security agencies exchange information with each other, you should also be careful with information about groups and individuals that are struggling against dictatorships. You should also be careful with sensitive address lists when traveling between countries. Some zealous customs officer can get the idea that her or his chief might be interested in them. Even if it can become necessary in certain cases to keep an investigation secret, it is important to make all controversial actions public as soon as possible. Giving others the opportunity to criticize and influence an activity while it is

still going on helps to maintain democracy and to avoid the
development of sectarian ethics.

CHAPTER III

EXPRESSIONS OF RESISTANCE: ABOUT ACTIONS

THE ACTION

I have always felt respect for the word "action." Actions were something other people did—not me. When I got involved in the nonviolence movement, I lost that respect, which was a good thing. You do *actions* every day.

As long as you are not living on a desert island, then you are politically involved. We work and consume and in this way keep the society going. Political actions are a part of our daily lives. Unfortunately, the political consequences of our actions are not always that positive. Since there is no such thing as a perfect system and the society is maintained by the daily cooperation between us as its members, then disobedience should be a daily activity.

One of the aims of civil disobedience is to enable us to lose respect for *actions*. Politics is not something that other people do on special, solemn occasions. Politics springs from our daily activities. The following two chapters about different forms of actions and how to practically go about doing an action are closely connected. Aside from describing actions and what these are aimed at, I will also discuss at whom they are aimed, and how it is possible with the help of symbols and action campaigns to communicate with the society and your opponent.

The Sanctuary Movement

Can refugees be granted asylum with the help of civil disobedience? Both those that have hidden refugees and those that make the decisions about asylum have had their doubts. A department head of the Swedish Immigration and Naturalization Service (INS) stated in a large daily paper that the INS was not affected by people who help immigrants by hiding them. But he gave perhaps too impervious an impression of the INS. In the autumn of 1988, I interviewed two acquaintances for a study about hiding refugees. Together they had hidden twenty-three people that were threatened with deportation. Only one of these, a refugee from Chile, was actually deported in the end, while the rest received residency permits. The officials of the INS are maybe not as inhumane as the department head seemed to want to imply. They become affected just like anybody else when people show solidarity. Both of my acquaintances told me that many police had shown solidarity. One of them was stopped as he was smuggling two Kurdish boys from Denmark to Sweden.

"If you have managed to take care of those boys this far, then you can probably take care of them in the future also," said the police and let them pass.

People that hide refugees in secret help many individual refugees to escape persecution and gain asylum. The problem is that hiding refugees becomes a solely humanitarian action. Since it does not become public, it does not affect the law and the application of the law to any great degree. The difficulty with civil disobedience, on the other hand, is that it is open. Refugees seldom want to risk being captured. Those that are deported can be persecuted and perhaps even killed. In order to avoid having to keep hiding refugees forever, the North American Sanctuary movement was founded at the beginning of the 1980s. This movement combines two traditions: to provide a sanctuary for refugees and to openly break unjust laws. The tradition of hiding refugees dates far back in history.

Central to the movement, therefore, is that a group openly provides sanctuary for one or more refugees who are threatened with being deported. They invalidate the decision to deport the refugee and make a new decision themselves. This action and decision is made public. At the same time, they negotiate with the authorities and try to bring about a mutual decision. The Sanctuary group has the responsibility of finding hiding places, keeping the refugees safely hidden, and supporting the refugees. This work is combined with different public actions.

Just a few years after this movement was founded, there were already about three hundred Sanctuary groups in the United States. Many were churches. But synagogues and solidarity groups have also openly provided sanctuary. In Sweden, the movement started in the spring of 1988; our first Sanctuary group was a local chapter of a labor union.

The modern underground railway is a movement in the United States that has close contact with the Sanctuary movement but that has not as yet come to Europe. During the period of slavery in the U.S., abolitionists had built what was called the *underground railroad*. These railroads, which consisted of networks of people and hiding places, helped slaves flee to the northern states. During the 1980s, this underground railway was rebuilt. Now people help refugees from Central America to escape to the United States or further to Europe and Canada. This movement is for the most part independent, but it works in close cooperation with the Sanctuary movement.

A friend of mine organized parts of the underground railway in New York State. She knew a farmer that promised to provide accommodation and work for refugees for short periods of time. Another person she knew had a car and offered to act as chauffeur. Somebody else offered a bed for a few nights. At the Canadian border, others took over and helped the refugees get visas and other documents.

People who are fleeing are nervous and run a great risk of disclosing themselves. It is easy to see when someone is afraid. The risk of making a mistake increases if a person is left alone, and it isn't a good idea for a refugee to get lost. That is why it is important for others to accompany them on trips or when they move to a new hiding place.

The risk of police arrest is greatest just when the decision to deport a refugee has been made, but it is difficult to know exactly when this decision is made. Several techniques can help a group find out when it is time for a refugee to go into hiding. One way is to have two refugees exchange accommodations. Another is to let a refugee live somewhere other than at the address the authorities have, while somebody from the support group lives at the refugee's official address. In both cases it immediately becomes known when the police start to look for the refugee.

The people who are hiding the refugee should not belong to his or her nearest group of friends or acquaintances, such as a relative or language teacher. It can even be dangerous if the refugee's friends or relatives know where his or her hiding place is. They are the first people that the police question and keep under surveillance.

People who are in hiding should always have addresses of alternative hiding places in case something happens while they are alone. Once the doorbell rang and the refugee, in the apartment alone, thought it was the police. He climbed out of the window and wandered around the city aimlessly until the group finally managed to find him again.

You should never let police that are searching for refugees into your home, not even if the refugees are hiding somewhere else. But we often want to show that we are innocent. If the police show up we feel we have to invite them in. This makes it easier for the police to figure out by deduction where the refugees really are. If the police force themselves in, you can call for witnesses. It is also possible to film the incident and make it public. To be on the safe side, it might be best to move the refugees that the police are actively searching for to another area until things calm down.

You should avoid having the address or telephone number of a hiding place on you or in your home. It is quite simple to use the telephone book instead or other similar address lists with many names on them.

The police can sometimes be a bit overzealous and bug telephones in an attempt to track hidden refugees. The name of the hiding place or the exact times of moves to different hiding places should not be said on the phone. It can also be dangerous to telephone the hiding place. If you have to call the hiding place or discuss sensitive things on the phone, then you can always visit a helpful, law-abiding friend. There must be someone in your group of friends who isn't suspected of anything and whose telephone is guaranteed to be free of bugs. In detective movies the hero always calls from a telephone booth. This would probably work too, but it isn't very convenient. Though it is possible these days to quickly tap many different pay telephones at the same time, I hardly believe that the police use such resources to chase refugees.

Families that have to go to a public authority for some reason, like regular mandatory reporting to the police, should go separately and at different times. On one such occasion, a woman was followed when she left the police station. When her husband reported to the police both were taken into custody. Again, shadowing is probably not that widespread in these cases. If you suspect that someone is being followed, then you can use the methods I described earlier to expose it.

A wanted refugee who is alone is faced with a difficult dilemma if he or she has to go to a public authority. In Värnamo, Sweden, for instance, the police set a trap. The support group had new, important information about the refugee's case. In fact, they thought the new proof so strong that the police definitely would send the case back to the Board of Immigration. The police agreed with them, but they wanted the refugee to give them the documents in person. When he came to the police station two days later, they broke the agreement and arrested him. Immediately afterwards, he was deported without the documents ever being sent to the Board of Immigration.

Along with actually hiding refugees, work must of course be done on their cases. You may have to find a new lawyer who has more time and interest or get new documentation. The moral pressure on the authorities increases by doing actions that strengthen public support. Hunger strikes are a usual method among refugees. They are often desperate and terrified of being deported. A hunger strike may seem to be the last resort, but it is often interpreted as blackmail: "If you don't change, then I will die." A hunger strike can have a direct negative effect if the opponent becomes inflexible. A fast for a limited time is usually a more effective method. It communicates hope and determination to struggle rather than desperation.

Achieving agreements with the authorities can run into certain predictable obstacles. For instance, refugees often don't tell the whole story at the police interrogation. This reticence can be because they are trying to protect friends or relatives who are still in their home countries, or because they feel anxiety and/or shame. Refugees will often refuse to say that they have been tortured. Even more seldom will they show their torture scars. Refugees are fleeing from the police, and they are used to being suspicious of them, so sometimes refugees lie during police interrogations. If information gets out, then maybe their friends will be caught. In other instances they can be very shaken because they are on the run and so behave in a confused and contradictory way.

Additional difficulties that arise during interrogations stem from class and cultural differences. Refugees from poor countries can have been forced to flee because they have protested against an official or employer. In such cases, they might not have been active in an organization, and therefore are not especially politically educated. They simply do not confirm our own prejudices about how a refugee should think and act.

The same problem arises when somebody is forced to flee from his or her country because a relative has been politically active. While I was in Chile in 1988, some of my friends helped a family escape to Canada. The family's oldest daughter, who didn't even live at home, was politically active. She had a good network of contacts and got by just fine. But revenge is often directed at people who are not themselves active. The security police came now and then and mishandled her family, and even the maid; so they fled.

Legal work should concentrate on establishing exactly what has and has not happened. All facts that you want to come to the attention of the authorities should have documentation to back them up. This documentation can be about the refugees themselves, or be proof that the oppression that the refugees have been subjected to really does exist.

A common problem for refugee families is that they regularly need a dependable doctor. Children are always getting sick. Doctors can also be important when documenting the refugees' state of health. Naturally, the fear of being sent home doesn't improve their physical or mental condition. The isolation that comes with going underground increases the stress on the refugees. One of my acquaintances, who hides refugees herself, is of the opinion that families with children provide the ideal hiding places. There is always someone there who has a little energy and time to be social, and the likelihood that somebody is home if something happens is also greater.

People that have helped refugees once often want to continue working in the solidarity movement. That is why many of those that are active in the underground railway or the Sanctuary movement also work toward changing things so that others do not have to flee in the first place. One movement that tries to prevent war is called Pledge of Resistance.

Pledge of Resistance

In the summer of 1983, I moved to Syracuse, New York. At the time, many of us who worked with solidarity issues were convinced that the United States was going to invade Nicaragua. Before I left for the U.S., I discussed with many of my friends the possibility of preventing an invasion *before* it happened by using civil disobedience. It should be possible, I thought, to get a government at least to hesitate before making such a fatal decision. Just imagine if you could get enough people to openly promise to do civil disobedience if a superpower sent troops into another country!

Other people had been thinking along the same lines, and during the summer of 1984, Pledge of Resistance was founded by several solidarity and peace groups together. Thousands of people sent written pledges to the White House stating that they promised to do civil disobedience if the U.S.

invaded Nicaragua. Some planned to occupy their local representatives' offices, while others intended to occupy military training bases. Local Pledge of Resistance groups were formed, and within a couple of years more than thirty thousand people had promised to go to jail if it was necessary to protect Nicaragua. Every time Congress increased funding for the contras, the U.S.-backed guerrillas, the network was activated. On several occasions, thousands of people were arrested. If the U.S. had actually invaded Nicaragua, the government would have been faced with a disobedience campaign that would have made the Vietnam War protests seem modest by comparison. A council consisting of representatives from different movements was established that could activate the network on a national level. The documents in which people promised to do civil disobedience were sent to a central address and copied before being turned over to the authorities.

On the local level, affinity groups and coordination councils were established that had complete freedom to do actions when they thought it necessary. The most important organizational work was to establish affinity groups and train everybody that had signed the pledge. Nonviolence training was absolutely necessary to keep the campaign from degenerating.

Early on in the Pledge of Resistance campaigns it was discovered that it was not a good idea to use the network either too often or too seldom. Either way the movement would be weakened. Thus, this method cannot be used exclusively, but should be combined with other forms of resistance.

The idea of a pledge of resistance is perfect for the solidarity movement. The Western superpowers have multinational corporations spread all over the world. These corporations and embassies are conceivable action targets when the superpowers escalate oppression in a particular country. Some people may think that it is difficult to do actions in democratic countries that draw attention to the oppression in dictatorships. But don't believe that! Even these countries have activities in democracies that are suitable targets for civil disobedience. One clear example is international trade. A variation on this method is to pledge resistance if a particular activity does not stop within a certain amount of time. This approach is also useful in movements other than the solidarity movement, for example in the struggle against environmental destruction.

Plowshares Actions

The Plowshares movement can be defined as a campaign to disarm weapons and challenge others to do the same. Plowshares actions have been inspired by a couple of Jewish prophets, Isaiah and Micah, that lived around 700 B.C. The prophets were a group of people who, based on their interpretations of reality, anticipated how the future would develop. By doing dramatic and often bizarre actions, they tried to communicate what needed to be done in order to set things straight. They preached justice and struggled against injustice. Seen as agitators who criticized the authorities and the people, they were therefore imprisoned and executed by those in power, or lynched by the people. The prophet movement became more established with time, and prophets began to represent the authorities or public opinion. Today, the duties of the prophets have been taken over by the peace and environmental movements. According to tradition, the prophets Isaiah and Micah are associated with optimistic visions of a just society. Isaiah said, "They will beat their swords into plowshares and their spears into pruning hooks. Nations will not take up sword against nation nor will they train for war anymore."[25] Micah adds that everyone will "sit under his own fig tree, and no one will make them afraid."[26]

Seven prerequisites for justice and peace can be identified in these two texts. By using different symbols, we emphasize them in our actions:

1. *Destruction of weapons.* Most groups limit disarmament to a few parts of a weapon. This is to inspire others to continue disarmament. A limitation is a symbol for the message: "We alone cannot reach a definitive disarmament; your help is needed."

After they disarmed a Bofors cannon in Sweden, two Plowshares activists received a critical letter from a woman who was peaceworker. She was disappointed that they had disarmed only one cannon. Why hadn't they rendered harmless all five cannons that were on the premises? Her reaction is the first half of what is needed for disarmament. Disarmament will become a reality when she understands that it is impossible to give the entire responsibility to others. A Plowshares action must be incomplete to prevent us from perceiving Plowshares activists as our proxies.

Once, however, a nuclear weapons silo was made totally useless by an action. Another time a group that called itself Avco Plowshares disarmed computers with a hammer, and the development of a newer, more effective nuclear weapon was delayed. The conclusion of these actions is obvious: we the citizens can, as a matter of fact, start disarming.

2. *Creation of something that feeds people.* We emphasize the constructive aspects of the action rather than the destructive ones by using common hammers to disarm. We also use symbols that represent the value of life and our prospects for caring instead of killing. For example, a Swedish Plowshares activist, Stellan Vinthagen, planted a tree during a disarmament action in Germany.

3. Not using violence.

4. That we shall not even learn how to use violence.

5. That we shall not prepare ourselves for war. Nonviolence is the foundation of every Plowshares action. That is why it is necessary to disarm ourselves as individuals and as a group, and to disarm the violence in our society.

6. Every individual must also have access to food. Peace implies that everybody's basic needs, such as food and shelter, are being met. Justice and peace are mutually dependent.

7. Finally, that we shall not be afraid of other people. By remaining at the site of the action, we intentionally make ourselves vulnerable to the law and our fellow beings. In this way we try to overcome fear, a fear that otherwise would cause us to protect ourselves and arm ourselves against others.

Of course, these aspects of work against violence do not cover the entire aim of a Plowshares action, nor all the symbols that are used. In order to give a complete description of each action, I would need to write a book about each one. Plowshares groups actually do publish their own books so that people other than judges, prosecuting attorneys, workers, and military personnel have an opportunity to gain insight into the action and discuss its message. Films have even been made about some actions. The most important media to spread the dialogue to a wider circle, however, are personal contacts, conversations, and invitations to new disarmament actions.

Disarmament

Perhaps the most controversial aspect of a Plowshares action is the destruction of weapons. There are many reasons why the movement makes tangible disarmament a priority.

During the spring of 1987, I interviewed several representatives of the opposition, so-called dissidents, in Hungary. Most of them had something in common, in that they worked specifically with two questions: freedom of speech and the right to make a living. They supported self-employed people, for example. Their struggle was always directed toward the people. If everyone said what they thought then freedom of speech would become a reality, no matter what the law said. As we have seen, the law later confirmed the right that the people of Eastern Europe already considered to be theirs. It isn't difficult to see a parallel between the dissidents' methods to get free speech and the Plowshares movement's endeavors to get people to disarm weapons.

However, my intention with this example is rather to emphasize the difference in capitalist countries. In a society where the state seeks total power, as in the former Soviet Union, an activist's basic struggle is to break down this total domination of the people. Our societies, on the other hand, are pluralistic. Power is divided up between different institutions, like the state and private companies, and no institution claims to have complete control.

There is another crucial factor that differentiates capitalist societies: private property. The right to private property is a principle holier than the value of the individual. The right to private property includes the right to buy other people's labor and thereby gain ownership over the results of their work. This means that I can sell my ability to work and make things, and then it is no longer mine. During a certain amount of time each day I am not allowed to make decisions about my own ability to work. I also renounce participation in deciding how what I produce will be used.

Two questions are important in capitalist societies: who controls the work and who controls the results of the work? Solidarity, peace, and environmental work are all concerned with these questions about right livelihood and the right use of resources. The capitalist principle of personal property has taken these questions away from the public sector and placed them instead in the private or business sector. The participant's right to have a say in decisionmaking and democracy is replaced by the question of ownership. The most cynical illustration of this is the production of weapons. The right to private property—weapons in this case—is more important than the right of those people being shot at to participate in decisionmaking!

Even state property is removed from the public sector and treated like private property. The democratic set of decisions only set the conditions for an activity. The actual use of resources is transferred to institutions and profit-making businesses. Anybody who doesn't believe me can test this by a simple experiment: try collecting your neighbors and go make the local post office nicer to be in during those long waits to get to the window.

When the State Railroads closed several stations in Värmland, in the middle of Sweden, the train conductors took the side of the passengers. They stopped at the old stations whenever anyone wanted to get off or on. The conductors were informed by the State Railroads that the people directly affected by the decision to close the stations had no right to make a different decision concerning how the *state's* trains should be used. In spite of this, the conductors continued to provide this extra service and finally the State Railroads was forced put the old train stations on the timetables again.

At her trial, Elizabeth McAlister from the Griffiss Plowshares Group attempted—until she was stopped by the judge—to show how weapons in our Western societies are considered divine. This holy, destructive property is mystified and considered more important than the individual. Weapons today function as modern golden calves or idols. This is made obvious when weapons manufacturers give their products names like The Body of Christ and Trinity. Reverently, we let these creations control our lives, and the value of property becomes greater than the value of human life. When a few almost embarrassingly amateur women and men with paltry hammers tear down these most holy objects and make scrap out of them, then the weapons are demystified. It is impossible to worship or even use a broken cannon.

This effective dethroning of weapons does not necessarily mean that destruction per se is a useful method in creating a better society. Disarming weapons is a careful, creative process, one that is useful in rendering harmless objects that could otherwise be used to hurt people. Vandalism, on the other hand, is an expression of frustration and inability to direct the struggle at the problem. Resistance must be understandable, function as an appeal, and focus on the problem.

Blockades

When I drag myself out of bed in the morning, make breakfast, and open the morning paper, I often read about civil disobedience. It never ceases to amaze me that these actions are almost always blockades. In Chile, members of Sebastian Acevedo block police stations where people are tortured. Owners of small boats in Australia stop nuclear-armed vessels from entering their harbors. A group of mothers and children blocks the entrance of a German nuclear weapons base. Greenpeace divers jump into the water in front of the Swedish nuclear-waste transport ship, Sigyn, and stop it from taking on cargo. People hug trees to protect forests in the U.S., Sweden, India, and Nepal. People in wheelchairs try to get into inaccessible restaurants and in doing so intentionally block the automatic doors.

The attempts to vary this form of action have been very creative, and in certain situations it is a very effective form of action. Unfortunately, however, there is also an unimaginative obsession with blockades in particular. When people decide to do civil disobedience, the first thing they do is block something. One-sidedness is never a good idea. The authorities often try to tone down the attention created by civil disobedience. The symbolically low fines solemnly demanded of the proud blockader are hardly a deterrent. If the authorities just shrug their shoulders, then a blockade as an action becomes pretty useless. Instead of creating a dialogue, the result is an indifferent silence. In Scandinavia blockades are often ignored, which is why they do not work as well there as they do in Germany and the U.S.

The myth that a blockade is less symbolic than other forms of civil disobedience has often created conflicts. To link arms or use chains usually prolongs the blockade for only a few minutes or at most a day or two if up to a thousand people participate. Chains also tend to reduce an affinity group's flexibility. They can cause problems if something happens that makes it necessary to break off the blockade quickly, such as if a sick person needs to pass. Activists can have a hard time of it if the police use water cannons, clubs, or tear gas and the person who has the key runs away.

Blockades are also often a very difficult and sometimes dangerous form of action. In the first place, physical hindrance can cause people to become frustrated. To force workers to climb over your body to get past can be interpreted as very moralizing. This can create a mental block in the people that you want to reach the most.

At the blockades I have participated in, several further problems have arisen: Should we also block the people coming out of the building or military base? Is it nonviolence to keep them shut in, even if the blockade is more psychological than physical? Who should we let through: ambulances, school buses, those that are not involved in the activity that we want to block...?

Blocking vehicles is one of the more advanced and dangerous forms of civil disobedience. The vehicle itself increases the anonymity of the driver, which can cause him or her to drive through the blockade. In September 1987, a train loaded with weapons bound for Central America was driven over the activist Brian Willson. The conductor did not slow down as he had at previous actions. The other participants jumped out of the way. But not Brian Willson. He survived but lost both legs. In spite of this, the action strengthened his commitment to a "nonviolent revolution." The revolution will demand its price, he says, which will sometimes be quite high. He continues to challenge others to overcome their fears.[27] Surprisingly enough, the result of this incident was that more and more people participated in the so-called Nuremberg actions at the California Naval Weapons Station.

The morally difficult question is if you should, in a similar situation, abandon the blockade and let the train pass. If an affinity group decides that they will break off a blockade, then they have to be sure that everybody can get out of the way. If just one person moves out of the way then the conductor can misunderstand the situation and think, "If I just keep driving then they will move." Either everybody or nobody has to move. But can you really be sure that everybody will have time to move? Even if you can be sure, what happens if another affinity group at a later action decides to stay put? The first affinity group has shown the conductor that it is OK to cold-bloodedly drive through the activists. This is why getting out of the way is not an alternative. At a vehicle blockade the opponent must be able to depend on the participants to keep their promise. This means that everybody must be prepared to be run over if necessary. Otherwise they should not be participating.

The risk of being run over can of course be reduced by physical barriers or by negotiations with the opponent in advance. A well-prepared blockade can work. However, this type of action is so difficult that it should not be the first choice when a group decides to use civil disobedience. Occupation, a closely related form of action, is often more useful.

Occupation

Occupation occurs when an affinity group enters an area where some kind of destructive activity is going on. One of the largest peaceful occupations ever carried out was in the U.S., in the Nevada desert area used for nuclear weapons tests. During a period of ten days, between March 11 and March 20, 1988, at least 2,065 people were arrested. It was estimated that about twice as many participated in the action.[28] In Latin America, homeless people regularly occupy areas. Within a couple of days several hundred poor people can build shacks on an abandoned field. The authorities are now accustomed to poor people's taking the initiative and making demands. If they throw them off the property, then another area is occupied and the struggle continues.

Occupation is often a flexible form of action. Depending on how the area is blocked off and how many get arrested, the occupation can be moved or reinitiated at new places and times. The most common mistake is that the affinity group does not give the occupation any meaning. In other words, occupation for the sake of occupation is not especially meaningful—it becomes downright boring. Only when it is combined with theater, poetry reading, or other kinds of symbolic actions does it become powerful. In Sweden, for example, with the help of local farmers, peace workers cultivated artillery ranges. In England, women decorated a military base with symbols for life.

Another common mistake is to not put a time limit on the action. At a sit-in in the turbine room at the Ringhals nuclear power station in southern Sweden, the activists said that they would sit there until nuclear power was shut down for good. "Well," the personnel answered, "just go ahead and sit here until it is!" Toward evening, the group decided to give up.

You never know if you are going to be arrested or not. The action must be planned in such a way that it is successful both if the activists are being arrested and if they are being ignored. One way of doing this is to separate the goal of the action from the long-term goal. The goal of the action can be, for instance, to build a windmill inside a nuclear power plant in two hours. The long-term goal can be to replace nuclear power with renewable energy sources. At another action at the Ringhals nuclear power station, we managed to build a windmill. If the guards had tried to stop us, their action would have been an important contribution to the symbolism.

An occupation can, in practice, function as a blockade. Safety regulations can stop a certain activity as long as unauthorized people are on the premises. Many nuclear weapons tests have been stopped this way. The advantage here is that the employees are not physically hindered from doing their work as they are by a blockade, which increases the possibility of starting a dialogue with them. An occupation can, however, be combined with smaller blockades of machines, for example. A blockade like this is more focused than a blockade of a building or an area since it is limited to a certain activity. The workers and others can freely move around the area.

Camps

Temporary or more permanent camps are one interesting form of occupation that has become popular during the 1980s. These camps are usually built beside a place where an unjust activity is going on. The most well-known example is the women's camp at a nuclear weapons base in Greenham Common, England. Less well known are some one hundred peace camps that at different times have been built at military bases in Europe and the U.S.

The camp idea is better established in the U.S. than it is in Europe. During the eighties in the U.S., it seemed to have gone so far that every base worth its name had to have at least one peace camp on its record. In the mid-1980s, anti-apartheid camps were set up all over North America as a protest against support of the white regime in South Africa. In Sweden, we have combined disarmament actions and camps. During the summer of 1992, a disarmament camp was set up at a military arms factory with the purpose of dismantling machines and disarming weapons.

The most important purpose of a camp is to establish an ongoing dialogue with the opponent. This kind of resistance is useful when opinions are polarized and the opponent has strong support. The Women's Peace Encampment at Seneca Army Depot in New York State, for example, was built in an area where a large part of the population worked on the base. The atmosphere was tense. The police even caught a man trying to chase the women away with a rifle. But with time, contact was established and people working on the base started giving tips to the women. When I participated in an action there, six months after the camp had been established, we were able to have long conversations with the flag-waving counterdemonstrators with no problems.

The most important thing is to show respect for the people living in the area. The Women's Peace Encampment had problems with women who intentionally provoked the local people. One thing they were successful with was training all the new women that were constantly arriving. The training covered subjects like civil disobedience, methods for holding a meeting, homophobia, feminism, and local history. The camp also printed its own fifty-page handbook called *Women's Encampment for a Future of Peace and Justice*.[29] In the U.S., it is actually quite common to print a handbook for every big action.

Conscientious Objection

Civil disobedience is usually well prepared. Actions are done by citizens who want to develop democracy. It is not, however, only as citizens that we need to develop democracy. As wage earners, we have just as great a responsibility to create democracy. One form of civil disobedience that can be completely spontaneous is conscientious objection.

Peter Cederqvist is a good example of this kind of conscientious objection. He has a family, and until the autumn of 1988 he was a driver for ODAB, a Swedish oil wholesaler owned in part by the cooperative OK.[30] Peter was absolutely not an activist. "But of course, things happened sometimes that made me think. One night my son Jon, who is three years old, wanted to hear a story about how people hug trees and when the machines come...." So even before that Friday in September, Peter supported the tree-huggers' attempts to stop the building of a highway through the forests along the west coast of Sweden.

One day, he was told to drive his tanker to JCC-Hammar. "My Volvo F10 was loaded with 4,000 gallons of diesel fuel and I drove northwards, along the coast to the city of Stenungsund," Peter recounts. But there were problems with the job from the beginning. Nobody knew where JCC-Hammar was. Peter asked at the local gas station and at the church. "I asked people in the area, but nobody knew where it was and finally I decided to go home. But on the way home I suddenly saw a sign with 'JCC-Hammar' on it and I was glad that I'd finally found the place." In the construction area a man confirmed that it was indeed JCC-Hammar and showed Peter the tank he was to fill. "I asked him what they were building," Peter says. "And I thought, if it is the new coastal highway then they are not getting any oil from me."

"We are building the new highway," the man answered.

"Unfortunately, in that case I can't let you have the oil."

Three days later Peter Cederqvist was called in by his boss and given an ultimatum—either obey orders or resign. The boss wanted Peter to take the initiative. Peter decided to quit.

A friend from Argentina, Nestor Verdinelli, who is a refugee counselor at a school in my home town of Gothenburg, returned the initiative in a similar situation. He had helped refugees in ways that were not included in his job description. The school principal asked him to come to her office and told Nestor that he would have to restrict the refugees extra help to his free time or resign. Nestor answered that he did not have two consciences, one at work and one at home. And he had no intention of quitting. The principal had a hard time taking action. Maybe she had no real reason to fire Nestor, or maybe she didn't really know whether Nestor was doing the right thing or not. Nestor still has his job and continues to provide support for refugees who need help.

Conscientious objection can be well planned and work in the same way as civil disobedience. One day Lars Falkenberg, a train conductor, was painting banners. Lars had been tipped off by a couple of switch-tenders that he would be driving arms to a harbor for export that night. He invited some of his friends over and we went to his place of work together. When we arrived, he connected the weapons cars to the engine but refused to drive the train. Instead he sat down on the tracks in front of the train.

Conscientious objection is an open refusal to obey orders or do what the law dictates. Usually it is an objection to compulsory military service or a refusal to pay military taxes. Conscientious objection has therefore mostly been used against state directives. During the past few years, however, it has become more and more common to take one's conscience to the workplace. During the winter of 1989, several telephone company employees in Norway refused to install telephones at the South African consulate. They were supported by the local chapter of their union. In Gothenburg, Sweden, harbor workers have refused to load arms.[31] They were also supported by their union. In another case, a chief of police refused to deport a refugee that he thought should be allowed to stay.

The most exciting aspect of this workplace development is that several unions have begun to support conscientious objection. Historically they have, unfortunately, often turned against the conscientious objector and taken the side of the company instead. Unions are now even giving courses in civil disobedience, at places of work, during business hours. Such a course can also be included in a vocational education program, as the school for welfare workers in Gothenburg has done.

Conscientious objection should in no way be confused with getting out of certain duties on the job. Objection is always public. This openness means that your action, which was perhaps at first founded on a private, moral conviction, becomes political. Changing jobs to avoid being forced to do what you consider wrong should also not be confused with conscientious objection. Changing jobs might be the best thing to do in certain situations, but the purpose of conscientious objection is either to assert your right not to do a certain job, or to completely stop that job from being done at all.

"Svejkism" is not conscientious objection. *The Good Soldier Schweik*, written by the Czechoslovakian author Jaroslav Hasek, has become a prototype for a kind of resistance based on acting simplemindedly.[32] By obeying orders or regulations literally, it often becomes impossible to carry them out. Too much enthusiasm can create just as much disorder as carelessness. When svejkism is not open refusal, then it usually doesn't change an activity. In spite of the fact that it makes an activity more difficult to do, it confirms obedience. If svejkism is done out in the open, then it can be a creative complement to conscientious objection.

Open conscientious objection, done on a large scale, is one of the most effective ways of creating a more just society. Just about all injustice is dependent on obedient wage earners. With a few exceptions, oppression is not done on a nonprofit basis. Therefore, one of the main intents of civil disobedience is to challenge people to be conscientious objectors. In order to do this, it is necessary to establish a relationship with the employees. This relationship should be begun before the action and maintained afterwards. If this interaction is neglected, then civil disobedience can, at worst, prevent a dialogue with the employees.

Before our Plowshares action in Florida, the peace group that later had the role of our support group distributed flyers at the entrances to the nuclear arms factory every week for a year. They continued to do this for several years after the action. Without these attempts to establish contact, the decision of the engineers and workers who later refused to manufacture nuclear weapons would probably have been much more difficult. Our support group also came in contact with a somewhat unusual conscientious objector. He was an infiltrator. On orders from the police, he infiltrated our support group and even chapters of the local union. He had misgivings, however, and after a few attempts at infiltration he told a newspaper about it. His disclosure was a minor scandal for the police.

Conscientious Objection to Military Service

The most common form of conscientious objection is refusal to do mandatory military service. Most conscientious objectors do it quietly. Their refusal would challenge more people if they sent out invitations to the trial or perhaps distributed conscientious objection handbooks to other people subject to the draft. Some friends got together and established an affinity group when one of them was drafted. The whole affinity group went with him to the military base. In this way, they could show that objection to military service was an issue that concerned both men and women. In addition, the group could provide the necessary support to the person who objected and even make contact with the soldiers on the base. Conscientious objection to military service can be done in several ways. Many just don't fill in the questionnaire from the military. Some people do not show up at the appointed time or refuse to cooperate at enrollment. It is also possible to wait until after enrollment. Some people have sent in a written statement saying that by principle they cannot cooperate with the military.

During a training course in civil disobedience for a writing course, I met the poet and ex-punker Jonas Wallgren. He had tried a very special form of resistance. Jonas was drafted on a beautiful May morning at the end of the 1980s. The depersonification process started immediately. During the two days of enrollment, everyone was forced to wander around half naked, with only their underwear on. Not only that, they were addressed by numbers. Jonas was called "210." But the commanding officer was faced with a problem. There was no one there that answered to "210."

Finally they corralled all the applicants into a big room. An intelligence test was handed out. But Jonas answered the opposite to all the questions. A corporal muttered something about a record being set. "This is the absolute lowest IQ-level ever!"

"The man giving the test got angry," says Jonas. "They grabbed me and threw me in a special room and put a thermometer in my mouth."

When he did the hearing test he didn't push the button, in spite of the screaming tone in his ears. "Do you know that you are deaf?" the doctor asked. No, Jonas hadn't known that.

"I have talked to a couple of friends that had done the same thing," Jonas recounts. "But I was scared anyway. I had never been so verbally abused before. More than once I felt like crying. The commanding officers made fun of me and my body. They said that I was a weakling and could understand why I didn't want to be in the military. They pushed me around and were aggressive. At night when everybody else went home, they locked me up. I had to nag my way out."

For some strange reason, Jonas was not allowed to talk to the psychologist like all the others in the group. "The commanding officers called me stupid and said, 'Your psychological problems are not of any interest to the military authorities.'" He was sent instead to a doctor and then to a chief medical officer. "Both doctors behaved in the same way. When I was called into the room they just stared at their papers for several minutes without addressing me. Then they looked up. I don't know if this was a conscious way of trying to break me down." The others in the group were afraid that something would happen to them because of Jonas's actions.

The group pressure was strong, and the commanding officer had strong control over the other boys.

Finally, Jonas was granted an exemption from military service. "Now, I am ashamed that I let them call me stupid. I should have openly refused instead of simply obeying. As it was, they thought I was trying to sneak out of doing military service." Jonas did his special kind of resistance against the draft. As I mentioned before, you do not have to show up at enrollment to announce your refusal. Many people write a statement to the authorities or an open letter to a newspaper and say that they refuse to cooperate with the military.

When I lived in Syracuse, New York, I participated in a support group for Andy Mager. He is one of the few people in the U.S. that has been punished for refusing to register for the draft. He traveled around to schools and groups that wanted to know how to refuse to register. Because he did this openly, he was given six months in prison. This way of choosing which people to punish has also met with resistance. Even women and senior citizens that do not have to enroll at all send in written promises to refuse to participate in the military system. This is also common in Spain.

The trial is an important forum to explain why you are a conscientious objector. It can also be a way for others that are thinking about refusing to get information. Therefore, the time and place for trials against conscientious objectors should be made public in peace magazines and other media.

Punishment also challenges friends and acquaintances to also work against militarism. It can be used in different kinds of actions. A Lutheran minister was imprisoned for conscientious objection to military service in 1982. He immediately started a fast to show that it was indefensible to imprison people who refused to cooperate with war. He was strongly supported, and after fifty-five days of fasting, he was released.

In Norway a group used ladders to break into a prison where a conscientious objector was imprisoned. The peace group then refused to leave the prison. Instead, these women and men demanded to be imprisoned as well, since they were also pacifists. When people *want* to be imprisoned, it becomes absurd to try to scare them with this kind of punishment.

Is It Sabotage to Wear Wooden Shoes?

Sabotage comes from the French word *sabot,* which means wooden shoe. Before the turn of the century, to sabotage meant working as though you had wooden shoes on—roughly, clumsily and sloppily. The word quickly gained an unexpectedly wide usage. Soon it meant such contrary actions as when business owners falsified their products or when workers intentionally used the best materials in spite of the fact that the orders came from poor customers. Later, sabotage gained a new meaning: destruction. Today most people associate it with bombs. Since bombs hardly can be considered nonviolence, there is nothing in this book about that. Instead I will discuss and criticize sabotage in its original meaning.

The productive Swedish writer Albert Jensen was the editor for a syndicalist newspaper. He wrote a couple of helpful essays on sabotage. The most comprehensive was published in 1912 and titled "What is Sabotage—An Investigation." He states here that the French workers Paul Delesalle and Emil Pouget introduced sabotage into the debate within the national union movement in the nineteenth century. According to Pouget, sabotage is a conscious practice of the maxim "Bad work for bad pay." This is intended to "hit the employer in his heart, that is, through the cash register."[33] When workers listen carefully to their boss or if they study business economics, they learn that labor is a product. Slowly something dawns on them. "Well, for a good price I can get a good product. If I don't pay very much then I won't get very much. Since I am badly paid, then I must make sure that my work is a bad product."

Sabotage within the workers' movement usually had two main forms: furnish bad workmanship, or reduce the profits that the company gets directly from the work. Bad workmanship usually affected the consumer. Not only that, the guilty party could easily be traced. So this method was not recommended. The intention was not to hit the client or consumer, just the employer's profits. On the other hand, a reduction of the speed of the work was seen as an effective method. The advantage with this method as opposed to striking was that the workers continued to receive wages during the negotiations. Persistent strikes were difficult to carry out because families risked starving. The intention here was to reduce profits to a minimum. Sabotage could also be used at the same time as strikes to stop strikebreakers from working. In such cases important machine parts were removed, making the machines unusable. Sabotage can also mean removing necessary raw materials. Then production cannot continue.

Another condition of sabotage is that it is done only occasionally and used only after the employer has refused to negotiate. Large companies complain sometimes that workers work as slowly as possible. This cannot be called sabotage. It only leads to a constant increase in costs that the employer can calculate and then impose on the consumer. Only when sabotage is occasional does it lead to reduced profits, writes Jensen. Along with the sabotage, negotiations usually take place that can lead to an agreement. If the company does not want to negotiate, then the intent of sabotage can be to get the employer to start negotiating.

According to Jensen, sabotage provides several possibilities of reducing a company's profits. The shop assistant who is strictly instructed to measure on the short side sabotages whenever he or she gives the customer correct measurements. You can also start working more carefully. People who follow regulations and security instructions literally often have trouble keeping up with the foreman's time schedules. Jensen calls this kind of extreme zealousness obstruction.

Albert Jensen stated emphatically that sabotage is not a spontaneous, enthusiastic action or the result of a fit of rage. It must be an action of "reflective will."

Jensen thought that sabotage should be intelligent. Pure destruction or the manufacture of bad products only turns the public against the saboteurs. Sabotage works best when it cannot be classified as illegal. Then it is more difficult to punish the workers, and resistance can be more persevering.

According to Jensen, people who criticize sabotage use bourgeois moral standards. He justifies sabotage as a means to the goal of a high social order without exploitation and injustice. But this position is misleading, for the end cannot justify the means. And a bourgeois morality cannot be criticized just because it is bourgeois; these are socialist clichés. Liberal principles that could be accepted today by the United Nations, such as human rights, are necessary and a good thing. The idea of the individual's inviolability is firmly established in the bourgeois tradition. This traditional strength is particularly important in preventing a morality that allows the end to justify the means. These principles must also be applied when judging sabotage.

Personally, I do not think that the method of sabotage is especially useful in industrialized democracies. The basic idea is to reduce profits without being discovered. Working in a sloppy fashion is a confirmation of obedience and fear of punishment by the opponent. An open noncooperation has greater possibilities for breaking blind obedience and challenging others to do likewise. Sabotage can be useful, perhaps, when the risk of doing civil disobedience is so great that it makes civil disobedience difficult to organize. Even Albert Jensen's essay is an expression of obedience. He writes, "It is not my intent in the following pages to spread propaganda, to praise criminal acts, to promote the use of sabotage, to recommend anything."[34] He was of the opinion that the main advantage of sabotage was the fact that it wasn't public disobedience but rather a reduction of profits to start negotiations.

But how are you supposed to negotiate when your sabotage isn't done out in the open? Then somebody has to represent the anonymous workers. Of course, representatives can be chosen. The discussion as a whole would, however, be democratic only as an open dialogue where everybody participates and contributes.

In the end, the principles of sabotage and civil disobedience are in opposition to each other. Civil disobedience can include, however, certain methods that are similar to sabotage. The Plowshares movement disarms weapons, but they do it in the open. Employees can choose to openly improve the quality of the products they produce against the orders of the employer. A worker or an affinity group can choose to take apart a machine that is intended for destructive activity.

Monkeywrenching

Monkeywrenching is a form of sabotage that has been used more and more on the West Coast of the United States since the end of the 1970s. Environmental groups like the Bonnie Abbzug Feminist Garden Club and the Fox use the simplest tools possible when they make environmentally destructive machines useless or when they spike trees to make them useless for the forest companies. Eco-defense or ecotage (sabotage to protect the environment) is used to mean more or less the same thing as monkeywrenching.

For several years the North American eco-defense movement was infiltrated, leading to several arrests at the end of the 1980s. One of the people arrested, Dave Foreman, is an editor of a handbook on monkeywrenching.[35] He is emphatic that the method is based on non-violence. He does not use the concept of nonviolence to mean a constant struggle against violence on all levels, as the nonviolence movement does. He means non-violence as without violence toward human or other life. Monkeywrenching is, according to Foreman, not a revolutionary method. Its goal is not to overthrow a political or social system. The method is quite simply a form of nonviolent defense of nature. A contributor to the handbook, Edward Abbey, defends the method as morally and legally legitimate. When somebody vandalizes your home, you have both the right and the responsibility to prevent the destruction. Nature is our true home, and it should not be devastated, but protected.

Eco-defenders choose each target and time of action carefully. The method is not used during important political negotiations that can lead to environmental protection. In addition, aimless vandalism is considered counterproductive. Foreman shows that vandalism destroys support from other citizens.

Eco-defense cannot be used together with civil disobedience, either theoretically or practically. It would obscure the open struggle that is built up over time. The participants do actions in secret, and therefore do not take legal responsibility for their deeds. This secretiveness is perhaps the method's weakness. Another contributor to the handbook, T.O. Hellenbach, states that the method is effective because it makes it expensive to destroy the environment. The profits from environmentally destructive projects are reduced when machines have to be fixed or when new machines have to be rented. The profit margins are small, and the knowledge that destruction of the environment can be expensive reduces investors' interest.

Insurance companies often pay the reparation costs. Repeated eco-defense can therefore increase the insurance costs of the destruction of sensitive natural areas. Other additional costs are increased expenses for guards and security controls. Subcontractors and other companies might hesitate to participate in projects that can cause them, too, to be subject to monkeywrenching.

Eco-defense in the North American form is above all an economic method of struggle. This emphasis on economics causes an essential flaw in the method. The goal should really be a broad *cooperation* to save the environment. As long as a relatively large part of the local population—at least a few tenths of one percent would be needed—does not participate in the struggle, then eco-defense can hardly be effective. Until there is a greater participation, this method survives under the same conditions as civil disobedience. Its effectiveness is determined by the possibility of establishing a functioning dialogue. If the actions prevent this, then the effect becomes directly negative. A secretive eco-defense where the participants do not take responsibility for their actions does not have in our culture any possibility of establishing either a positive dialogue or broad cooperation.

CHAPTER IV

THE VOICE OF RESISTANCE: ABOUT THE ACTION

THE OPPONENT

"In war you fight the enemy. In politics you compromise with them." This rhetoric does not help us to understand either politics or war. But it might help us to understand pacifists' abhorrence of the concept of "the enemy." The Prussian military theorist Carl von Clausewitz stated in 1831 in his classic book that war is a continuation of politics, just by other means.[36] This is certainly true for many political systems, but it doesn't have to apply to all. Unfortunately, it seems to be true for our industrialized, capitalist system. Nonviolence nevertheless is an attempt to relegate Clausewitz to the dustbin, though we often tend to do the opposite when pacifism becomes passivity. Nonviolence is a way of *acting*. It is action.

Violence and passivity are two sides of the same problem. When we are passive we actively participate in oppression. We confirm its main condition—obedience. Even those in the rich parts of the world who actively struggle against violence participate in the oppression that we either subject the rest of the world to or indirectly support. We are political beings and therefore responsible. That is the way it is.

In civil disobedience, no enemies are proclaimed. The actions are, however, directed at somebody. Who is the opponent, then? In nonviolence, you include yourself as an *opponent*. It is impossible to make a self-righteous separation between us and them. Our struggle cannot be interpreted only as the struggle of the oppressed against the injustice of others. We cannot see ourselves as the representatives of *the oppressed*, either. Our struggle is always a struggle even against ourselves. This responsibility of ours absolutely does not mean that we are all equally responsible. We are not all involved in the same way in everything that is happening. This does not, however, relieve us of this responsibility. We not only have responsibility for our own actions, we also have responsibility for the actions of others.

Our actions become political when we understand that the struggle is not just about cleansing ourselves of our own sins. Our responsibility is quite simply to stop injustice and violence. It is a delusion to think that I have done my part just because I have disarmed nuclear weapons and gone to prison for it. Militarism is still going strong and I have just as great a responsibility as before to stop it.

Different groups have different possibilities. Actions should help to realize these possibilities. But first we have to know who we are talking to, that is, to whom the action is directed. I call these *dialogue partners* or *opponents*. The four main dialogue partners in civil disobedience are:

- The main opponent, who is the consumer and the taxpayer, i.e., ourselves. Our obedience is the prerequisite for the power structure of the industrialized world.
- The workers who directly participate in the activity that an action is directed against.

- Those who are in command at a worksite and who make the decisions.
- There are also people who have a control function. These are our friends, relatives, colleagues, employers, police, judges, lawyers, district attorneys, and ourselves through our own self-control and distaste for causing trouble.

An action does not, of course, have to be directed at all four target groups at once. The dialogue partner at one action can be the taxpayer and at another, representatives of the law.

The opponent functions mainly in two ways: to provide the necessary resources to keep a certain unjust activity going, and to control people who might try to obstruct the activity. These are very concrete functions. Civil disobedience is based on the possibility of creating a practical cooperation that can stop oppression and create justice. The condition for cooperation is a dialogue. In the following sections, I will describe civil disobedience as a way of creating dialogue and cooperation.

Resistance Campaigns

As I have indicated earlier, an action consists of much more than breaking the law. The preparations and follow-up work with the trial and invitations to new actions together form a whole. We can perceive civil disobedience from an even more holistic perspective. Several actions build up a campaign. A resistance campaign includes both legal and illegal actions. Every new action strengthens the effect of earlier actions. You could even say that old actions come alive again through a continued resistance. Earlier actions cause the effects of subsequent actions to become stronger than if they had been isolated actions. One plus one is more than two. Unfortunately, the opposite is also true. A bad action can destroy earlier or future actions.

It is not, however, the number of actions that determines a campaign's effectiveness. The strength of the moral challenge at every action is decisive in how the action will affect the campaign's results. Gandhi showed that a campaign needs to escalate so that it doesn't lose its effect. I would like to add that some "first steps" should be included during the entire campaign in some form. In other words, at every phase there should be a possibility for new participants to escalate their own participation. Some forms of action might not have the same political effect as before. A change in the behavior of obedience can nevertheless be more important in the long run than the direct political effect of an action.

The actions that lead to maximum punishments do not necessarily cause greater effects. It is the interplay between the moral challenge, which lies in the conquering of fear, and the dialogue created as a result of the action that decides its effect. The message of resistance needs a forum where it can be questioned, or otherwise it just becomes pacifying agitation and propaganda. By having dinners and parties, direct contact can be created with opponents and citizens. This contact is a prerequisite to keeping the dialogue going. During the course of the campaign, friendships between the different sides can develop. These friendships can then lead to cooperation. An isolated action is just the beginning of a dialogue. The aim of the campaign is to complete the dialogue.

Symbols

In order to have a dialogue you need a common language. During civil disobedience this language consists, among other things, of symbols. *Symbolon* is Greek, and means sign. The French philosopher Paul Ricoeur shows that symbols have a double meaning:[37] on the one hand, a direct meaning, and on the other, an indirect meaning that can be understood only through the direct meaning. A symbol never stands only for itself. It always expresses something, but it is not only a sign that represents something else. It also represents itself. An action, then, has to achieve or accomplish something to be symbolic.

A symbolic action has a message that is greater than the action itself. It is, however, a direct action as well. Many people think, incorrectly, that symbolic actions and direct or effective actions are opposites. A symbol needs to be interpreted in order to become a symbol. If a direct action has a *meaning* it therefore becomes a symbolic action. It is possible to imagine an action that doesn't have any message at all. The struggle would then be complete when the action was over, i.e., there would not be any reason to inspire others to engage in resistance. But such an action exists only in theory. Even actions that achieve the intended goals have messages that are wider than the concrete goals themselves. If the action is effective on its own, then its symbolic value is substantially increased.

Symbols are constructed so that those toward whom they are directed can understand or recognize them. As a matter of fact, it is those who perceive the symbol who create the symbolism. To use symbols in civil disobedience is to invite the opponent to participate in the resistance. In this way, the *action* is actually created after the activity is over. In sum, actions can both be symbolic and actually achieve something. Passivity in the face of injustice is itself a symbolic action. The unconscious message in this action is: Be passive! Confirm the structure of power! At the same time, passivity is a realization of other people's power.

Even a realization of justice—for example, when a country in the Third World frees itself from a superpower and becomes independent—is a symbolic action. A revolution has a message for the rest of us in the world that is above and beyond the main intention of the revolutionary groups. This symbolic value provides the country with a certain protection against invasion by the superpowers. Modern weapons give the superpowers the ability to crush any Third World country, but extreme brutality on the part of a superpower risks destroying the support it needs. The superpower still needs support from part of the population during an occupation, as well as from large parts of the rest of the world. Terror should preferably not be seen. Or, if it is visible, it should be perceived as a natural answer to a few leftist fanatics' suppression of democracy and freedom. It was, for example, to a certain extent the symbolic value of the Nicaraguan liberation that prevented the U.S. from invading the country during the eighties.

Words become action when they are expressed. In the same way, an action becomes words when it is understood. To polarize words and action is misleading. The well-known slogan used by the resistance movement, "Turn words into actions," must mean to go from one word to another word or to go from one action to another. The point of the new action is to achieve what you have demonstrated for earlier. The realization of your goal can be factual *and* symbolic. An example of this is when citizens provide actual sanctuary for refugees that are threatened with deportation, instead of only demanding that they be granted asylum. The protest turns into a symbolic *and* real creation of a hospitable society.

The resistance movement often mistakenly does not understand the real value of an action. In the beginning of a disobedience campaign, actions function almost exclusively as symbolic actions. The value of an action, together with the trial and the following punishment, is its *message*. The message can be directed toward those in power, as in the case of some Greenpeace actions: "Follow our example, stop waste-dumping at sea." It can also be directed at the citizens, as in the case of Plowshares actions: "We have started disarmament. Continue to disarm!"

The fact that Greenpeace often succeeds in stopping particular waste-dumpings and the Plowshares movement actually does disarm weapons does not make the actions less symbolic. Quite the opposite—the symbolic value increases when you show the possibility of stopping waste-dumping and that everybody can disarm weapons.

At a certain point, which cannot be exactly pinpointed, civil disobedience becomes a resistance that is in itself realizing the goal. This kind of resistance of the masses, with perhaps thousands of participants, is not as dependent on the strength of the message of the individual actions. Gandhi's salt march, which I mentioned earlier, is the most well-known example of this kind of civil disobedience, where the resources of the authorities quickly became insufficient. Hundreds of thousands of Indians extracted salt from the sea, in spite of its being forbidden according to English law.

This massive disobedience—where several thousand people continuously participate—has different dynamics from civil disobedience. We do not have very much experience of this kind of *civil resistance* in the Western world during peacetime. Modern examples of it, such as the events in the Philippines during February 1986, in China in May 1989, in Eastern Europe in 1989 and 1990, and in the former Soviet Union in 1991, prove difficult to apply to the conditions of the Western world. However, in the Western so-called democracies it is usually sufficient if we seem to just come into the vicinity of this mass disobedience for the opponent to be affected and want a dialogue.

An example of a disobedience campaign that was successful thanks to its symbolic value was the struggle for the Kynne Hills on the border between Sweden and Norway. People guarded these hills day and night during the entire

1980s to stop exploratory drilling for final deposition sites for uranium waste. If the people who were watching saw drillers coming, they were to start a telephone chain going that would lead to an occupation of the place. Of course, the authorities could, by using all their resources, start drilling even if the whole area participated in the occupation. But the political losses for those in power would have been too great.

The struggle for the Alta River in Norway is an example where resistance failed because, among other reasons, too many participants thought that they could physically stop the damming of the river. More than a thousand people participated. While some chained themselves with strong chains to the mountainsides along the river, others chained their arms together inside of thick iron pipes, so that the police couldn't cut the chains so easily. With these methods a few hours were gained, but there was a net loss due to the great disappointment when people realized that it wasn't enough. According to the Norwegian professor Thomas Mathiesen, who analyzes power structures and was present at the Alta River protests, the effect would have been greater if they had temporarily retreated. With more imaginative actions they could have forced the government to keep its huge force of police and military troops back. Mathiesen recommends a method called political jujitsu. Jujitsu is a Japanese form of self-defense that is based on using the opponent's own strength against him or her. In the Alta River example, the battlefront could have been moved to the courts and the detention cells rather than the place of action.

The three symbols that form the nucleus of civil disobedience begin to take form here. Through an act of disobedience, the prerequisite for the opponent's power is removed: obedience. In the dialogue during the trial, one's own ethics and those of the opponent are tested against generally accepted ethics. The punishment after the trial becomes the moral appeal that challenges others to continue the resistance.

A good example of the symbolic dynamics of nonviolence is when senior citizens blocked the Pershing II base in Mutlangen, Germany, in the spring of 1987.[38] Right in the middle of the blockade, the troops started a huge maneuver, and several hundred senior citizens followed them. The German peace activist Tina Utermark reported later that there was great confusion among the soldiers. The procession of senior citizens that followed this secret NATO convoy started up discussions all over Germany. When the German authorities arrested the participants, more people got involved, and the resistance grew.

At the same base, a concert blockade was carried out in the autumn of 1986. A symphony orchestra stopped all activities at the base by playing classical music for a whole day. The authorities refused to arrest them. The musicians gave themselves "detention" and continued to play. During the following weeks the base was blocked by quartets and quintets that played Renaissance music. In this way, they finally got the authorities to open a dialogue with them when they were arrested and taken to court.

It is not only the activists' own actions, however, that have a symbolic value. To arrest people who appeal to other people's consciences, to try them, and to punish them is the opponent's contribution to the struggle. They push the question of obedience to the extreme. The interplay between the actions by the resistance group and those of the opponent challenges other people to actively take a stand.

If you plant grain, it hardly has a political effect. There is not much symbolic value in an arrest, either. But someone who is arrested for planting grain can reap a significant harvest. Symbols used in civil disobedience have an intent that is beyond the action itself. In Plowshares actions, we use hammers to disarm weapons. But they are just as much intended for the trial. You shouldn't be afraid to use symbols that are difficult to interpret. Symbols should provide the background for discussions. They help to deepen a dialogue. The risk in using superficial and simplified symbols is that the challenge also becomes superficial.

Paul Magno, with whom I did an action in Florida, tied pictures of children from his community for homeless families to his hammer. He did this so that they would end up in the district attorney's evidence. He wanted to explain why these homeless children needed the resources that were being used for the arms race.

Todd Kaplan tied to his hammer at the same action a piece of paper money that was printed by Jews in the Warsaw ghetto during World War II. Poland was occupied and the ghetto Jews were being taken in batches to concentration camps. In spite of this terror, the inhabitants tried to live civilized lives. Todd, who is Jewish himself, testified during his trial about how the old bill meant hope for him. We should be able, he said, to live normal lives without the threat of obliteration. The people who printed the bill had not become paralyzed by the terror that they were subjected to. We should not become paralyzed either; let us rather show how we want to live.

My hammer symbolized for me the paradox inherent in militarism. A Pershing II missile can annihilate my home town of Gothenburg, Sweden. There are no weapons that could stop such an attack. But my small, ridiculous hammer made it impossible to fire that particular missile. And similarly, it isn't raw strength that can stop the arms race—weakness is our means for disarmament. This might seem paradoxical. But disarmament must be done, and actions that are based on vulnerability make it possible. This idea directly confronts the emotion that creates violence and power structures: our desire to build walls of protection.

The arms race could not continue without the obedience of citizens, which is caused mainly by people's fear of the consequences of disobedience. But there are no functioning methods of control today that could be used against an entire population that is prepared to take the consequences of their disobedience. Therefore, vulnerability to the consequences becomes the prerequisite of breaking obedience's hold on us. There is no other way. What seems to be impossible becomes the only possibility.

Effectiveness or the Search for Truth

An interesting ongoing discussion within the Plowshares movement is about cause and effect. Is it possible to talk about effective Plowshares actions? If you want to measure the effectiveness of an action, then you assume that the change can be reduced to a mechanical cause and effect, i.e., "If you turn this cogwheel, then the other cogwheel moves as well." Many in the Plowshares movement assume instead that our society is so complex that what seems to be the effect of an action cannot be explained only by the action. Our actions do not function like a cue that hits a billiard ball that hits another billiard ball. In that case, we should be hitting the ball more accurately than the opponent in order to win the game.

Civil disobedience can hopefully be a challenge for others. But they decide for themselves what they want to do with that challenge. Take, for instance, the story I mentioned earlier about the employees that stopped working with the Pershing II after our Plowshares action in Florida. We can't congratulate ourselves for that. The effect of our action was completely dependent on how others handled it. Those workers decided to stop manufacturing nuclear arms. Other people's belief in the necessity of arms manufacture may have been confirmed as a result.

I do not mean that all actions are either just as good or just as ineffective. The goal must be to always do the right thing. During our search for truth, we should always ask ourselves what has to be done to reduce our oppression of the poor. These insights can then be used by others in their search. But even if we do an action that seems to be genuinely true, many people can still be unmoved by it or decide to actively fight against what we perceive as the truth. The effects are therefore difficult to predict. It is hard to isolate the direct results of an action.

Changes can sometimes be predicted without difficulty if a group clearly expresses its intent from the very beginning. This is also a cause and effect model, but this model is more like chess than pool. The cause is in the future after the effect, that is, in the goal itself. Finding the cause of this intent can, however, be very difficult. It can also be difficult to calculate what happens when others try to stop the group from carrying out their plans. With the help of power and game theory, you could try to calculate the balance of power and the conditions of a continued power game. But some members of the group might change their minds. Perhaps they suddenly see their goals are indefensible. Then you can no longer explain events with the help of the rules of the game.

Changes can also sometimes be predictable according to the structures in the society. The economics laws of our market system demand that all private corporations must strive for growth and maximum profits; otherwise, stock buyers would not invest in them. This makes the environment a lower priority for corporations. It is possible that a consumer's choice of products can force a company to show more consideration for the environment, but it is still profit interests that govern the company.

What happens when cooperative or nonprofit companies gain a greater profile in society? Some of these companies might adapt to a more profit-oriented business, but after a while other, "newer" laws of economics would start to apply. It would no longer be possible to explain a company's behavior as a search for maximum profits and growth. We would have a new economic system that could no longer be called capitalism.

If you don't believe that society is a billiard table or a chessboard, then it becomes difficult to talk about tactics and strategies. A tactician is helpless without accurate pool cues. What good is the truth if you want to get the last ball to roll into a hole? It is just in the way. A tactician needs the security of the rules of the game. He or she would just become confused if a king offered his life for a pawn. A tactician has to get all of the opponent's pawns. The day he or she begins to like one of these insignificant pieces, then he or she is out of the game.

For a tactician, the ends always justify the means. "If we keep a low profile now, we will a have better chance of affecting the situation at a later time," the tactician may argue. What ever happened to honesty? Communication demands sincerity. To conceal what you really think is dishonest and hinders a dialogue.

"If we hit them hard now, when the authorities have a lot of other problems, then they will not have as many resources with which to stop us. Then we are sure to win," states the tactician on another occasion. But who says that the solution is checkmate? Playing a game means obeying a certain set of laws that you can tactically use to beat the opponent. But civil disobedience is not a power game. It is a dialogue that should lead to agreement. If the common solutions seem remote, then the conditions for the abuse of power must be removed.

To tactically play one power against the other leads to increased armament, fear, and suspicion.

The strategist, on the other hand, forgets the daily troubles of life. These are to be solved in the far future through parliamentarism, revolution, general strikes, an ecological lifestyle, more women in politics, or whatever the strategic goals happen to be. But what does the strategist say about the people who are oppressed today? Perhaps the "big solution" is not the real solution. Perhaps that which is nearby and that which is far off are connected with each other. The most accessible solutions should also be those that are the best long-term solutions. Resistance should be connected to our history, to the present, and to the future. By being active, we create both a history and a future. My daily life is connected with world politics.

Guidelines for Nonviolence

The helicopter lowers slowly over the bridge. Suddenly it rises dramatically. It circles a couple of times. Soon it is out of sight. The first police cars arrive immediately afterwards. I have time to count eight cars and one bus. Then my attention is distracted by the police dogs. The dogs stare quietly and seemingly indifferently at us. About thirty police officers stand behind them. Most of them have put on white riot helmets. Many have their clubs drawn. This scene is from Landslide Bridge outside of Gothenburg in 1983, right downhill from my house. Because there were people on the bridge, it could not be opened. And it was therefore impossible for a Danish boat suspected of carrying a load of arms to pass through.

The police on the bridge had probably never intervened against civil disobedience. Later, due to the increase in civil disobedience during the 1980s, they probably had gained more experience. Everybody who has confronted frightened police in similar circumstances knows that the first contact has to give them a sense of security. They do not know what is going to happen, and are probably more nervous than the activists.

Even those that participate in an action need to feel a certain sense of security, perhaps not with the police but with the other activists. The participants can be children or senior citizens, experienced veterans or those that are doing civil disobedience for the first time. I am afraid of participating in actions if I do not know how the other activists are going to react. I need to feel that we can count on each other.

Both the civil rights movement and the Indian independence movement used *nonviolence guidelines* to create this sense of security. These guidelines were made public and created a mutual understanding between the police and the activists. Several of these original guidelines are still in use, and some have been added. Every guideline is based on an agreement among several affinity groups about the framework of the action. If you leaf through action handbooks, the following guidelines seem to be the most common today:

- Meet every person with the respect and politeness that you can expect from a new acquaintance.
- Do not use physical or psychological violence.
- Do not take weapons or any form of protection against violence with you to an action.
- Do not run.
- Do not use drugs.
- Everybody, even the support people, should be members of an affinity group.
- Everybody should have been through nonviolence preparation.

Several of these guidelines can seem to be self-evident. Unfortunately, this is not always the case. Often, different interpretations of what the affinity group agreed upon arise.

For example, discussions within the nonviolence movement have focused on whether shouting slogans should be considered psychological violence or not. Slogans can in any case create tensions and aggressiveness in both the opponents and the participants, so chanting is avoided these days. Two good alternatives are conversation and song. Running can also cause unnecessary tensions, and, at worst, panic. The same is true if drunk people act in an unpredictable fashion. Or, in spite of the agreement not to take weapons to an action, some people forget to leave their pocketknives at home. This can cause unnecessary rumors among the police and the mass media: "They were armed with knives...." The opponent can perceive tools or a glass bottle as potential weapons, which makes the whole situation more difficult. At Plowshares actions we use hammers. When the disarmament is completed, we place them on the ground to avoid provoking the police and guards.

At demonstrations in Europe, some people put on protective gear, like helmets or handkerchiefs tied around their faces. But nonviolence is based on the power that is created by making yourself vulnerable and by taking the consequences of your actions. These modern suits of armor do not have any role in civil disobedience. Of course, situations can arise in dictatorships, say, where one is not ready to take the consequences of an action. But then the method of civil disobedience is abandoned. Since nonviolence is not intended for heroes and martyrs, escape can be the necessary alternative to open disobedience.

Even if the consequences in more liberal societies are usually more endurable, every participant must still be very well prepared. After a few bitter failures, the Indian independence movement learned that everybody needs nonviolence training or some equivalent form of preparation before actions. This demand is still with us today. It comes back time and time again after repeated mistakes when there "wasn't time" for training.

After the great success at the Seabrook nuclear power plant in 1976, the demand that all participants in civil disobedience be members of affinity groups was established. This guideline provides a sense of security for everybody. If someone loses control, there is always a group that can help and provide support. It is important to take this demand seriously. If ignored, the development of civil disobedience can be impeded and the tendency can arise to return to forms of action that require strong leaders.

Guidelines other than the seven mentioned above can arise, of course, depending on what kind of action is planned. A frequent addition is: Do not destroy property.

When you participate in an activity, you should be able to count on the fact that nothing is happening in secret. Anybody who is thinking about participating should have the chance to take a standpoint on what the other affinity groups have planned before she or he makes the decision. This democratic demand should perhaps be added as a guideline at big actions.

Some people stubbornly insist that they alone are responsible for their actions and nobody else should be affected. But this is a delusion. Seldom am I the only one considered responsible for my actions. At a blockade of a Norwegian military airstrip, the participants were retained overnight, an unusual step. They couldn't understand why. The next day, during the court proceedings for the issue of a warrant of arrest, they found out the reason. The night before, the only Swedish participant had been inside the air base and removed a military instrument that he intended to use in a symbolic way in a later peace demonstration. The Swede was detained in an isolated cell for two weeks. The Norwegian participants were released after a night since they had not been involved in his action. The Swede's unexpected action caused disappointment and conflicts among the activists.

Thus, resistance can have consequences that affect people other than those that actually do the action. We also have a moral responsibility for each other. Civil disobedience should, if possible, be preceded by information to all participants, the opponent, and even other groups that are working on the same issue. This publicness provides the opportunity for those involved to give their opinions and possibly stop us from making fatal mistakes.

Arrest

"Unfortunately, I will have to carry you away from here. Is it OK if I take a hold of your jacket?" One of the first times that I participated in civil disobedience was in 1983. The police showed me by their correct behavior the way to a functional resistance. An arrest is a meeting between people who are usually strangers to each other. When people meet for the first time, it is not considered good behavior to start moralizing or preaching to each other. The first thing is to get to know each other. The message can be discussed later in the police car or during the interrogation.

In civil disobedience, there are no enemies. The police are, however, one of the opponents. In order to understand the dynamics of nonviolence better, you should separate the police's function of protecting an unjust activity from the person behind this function. In civil disobedience you appeal to the police as people and challenge them to refuse to obey orders and support the action instead.

Based on the assumption that disobedience is a meeting between civilized people, the activist often chooses to react in one of the following ways when she or he is arrested:
- Obey the orders of the police.
- Obey the police only when they intervene.

- Passive resistance or refusal to cooperate.
- Active resistance.

Contact with the police usually works best if you voluntarily accompany them right away or when they intervene. Refusal to cooperate should be used only when the action can thereby symbolically gain strength. If a part of the action has not yet been completed, for example, or in a blockade, such refusal might be your best course of action. Active resistance, like locking elbows or hanging onto something, can increase the frustration of the police. This method was used more during the 1960s and 1970s, when many people hoped that nonviolence could function as a physical means of showing strength. I do not consider chaining yourself to a fence active resistance. Then you are not using your own muscle strength. Chains are a symbol or a means, not a behavior.

Passive resistance can gain a strong symbolic effect when the police refuse to negotiate or when they use violence. Sometimes, however, refusal to cooperate is used automatically, without thinking. As with all other types of resistance, you should ask yourself what the intent is, and when a certain method should be used. Some people start cooperating with the police as soon as they are out of sight of the public or when they get into the police car. But why choose these particular points in time? Why not use passive resistance until you are released from the police station or until the police agree to negotiate? If you don't have a concrete reason for refusing to cooperate, then you should cooperate.

When contact is established with individual police officers beforehand, the risk of a brutal arrest is reduced. To reduce that risk even more, a support person can take responsibility for recording, either in written form or with a camera, the arrest of each member in the affinity group. This record also increases the possibility of locating each individual police officer if you need them as witnesses at the trial. The arrested person can ask who arrested him or her, at the police station, if the police haven't given the name already.

Before the arrest, it is important to empty your pockets of any sensitive addresses. A friend of mine forgot to do that once. He was arrested with the addresses of a large number of resistance activists in Germany, Holland, England, Norway, and Sweden on him. After his arrest, a peace researcher in Germany became a bit paranoid and thought he was under closer surveillance than usual. Two guard cars followed us around the Pershing II base in Mutlangen, Germany, when he and I were investigating the possibility of disarming a weapon there. Personally, I did not think it was all that strange that we were being so carefully watched. Both he and I had done civil disobedience before, and the fact that the police had a list of addresses probably did not make any difference. Luckily, those of us on that list work openly with civil disobedience. In some situations, for example hiding refugees, things like this simply must not happen.

Interrogation

The leader of the interrogation points out a chair. I nod politely and sit down. The spotlight blinds my eyes. Squinting, I try to look around. On the left is the notorious head of security that broke two fingers of a woman from the peace camp. Earlier he bent both my arms back and locked them with his long, thin wooden baton. Now he seems to have calmed down. Straight in front of me, behind that head of the interrogation, is the FBI agent. To the right are two people I do not know. They introduce themselves later as immigration police. Apparently, I am the only one who is allowed to sit.

"No trouble now. Tell us your name and who the others are."

"What happened to the woman you took away?"

"We ask the questions here...."

"Then I don't have anything to say at the moment."

One of the immigration police quickly bends forward and stares me right in the eye. "We have certain privileges, you understand," he says vehemently. "We can keep you here for fourteen years if you don't talk." The interrogation degenerated from there and became pathetic. I gave no information. None of the others allowed themselves to be interrogated. They finally got our names when somebody came up with the idea of reading our statement. Later we were thrown off the air base. The judge fined me forty dollars.

In Europe, the opposite problem usually arises. There, it is difficult to give information during an interrogation. The interrogation can theoretically be an important part of the action. It provides an opportunity to start a dialogue and document facts and opinions. The people responsible for the interrogation usually only reluctantly write down more substantial information when it is presented orally. It is therefore a good idea to take statements and fact sheets with you to an interrogation. Ask to have these appended to the minutes of the interrogation.

However, situations can arise where you do not want to provide certain information. Above all there are two factors that affect how much you should cooperate: 1) If you have certain demands, for instance to be allowed to contact fellow activists, you can refuse to participate in the interrogation until these demands are met. 2) If there is a danger of hurting others, you can avoid giving certain information.

Depending on these two factors and the aim of the action, you can choose the degree to which you cooperate:

- Complete cooperation. You quite simply tell the interrogators everything they want to know.
- Restricted cooperation. One basic rule is that you usually do not give information about other people, but let them provide information about themselves. Some

people never give their social security numbers, on principle.

- Noncooperation. Women from different peace camps, like the Women's Encampment for a Future of Peace and Justice, have in certain situations refused to cooperate with the police after being arrested. This decision is usually combined with some form of passive resistance.

All the information provided should be correct. Half-truths and lies destroy the possibility of creating a feeling of trust.

The problem is that for some reason it is easier to give incorrect information than to refuse to answer. Obedience is so deeply rooted that people want to at least be perceived as being obedient. They would rather lie than openly refuse. For instance, even at nonviolence courses during interrogation role-playing exercises, the participants have trouble keeping strictly to the truth. The following dialogue is from an exercise and is, if not representative, quite a common occurrence during courses:

"Do you know the people who distributed the flyers for you?"

"No!"

"No?"

"Yes, well I mean that I don't want to answer the question...."

"I only wonder if you know them?"

"Yes, well I guess I do...."

Honesty is the best way to avoid these kinds of embarrassing situations. When you hesitate before answering a question, you can take time to think or ask to talk with someone else from the affinity group. You can always ask to continue the interrogation later. Why not ask if you can be interrogated together? If the interrogators don't accept that, there is still always the possibility of breaking off the interrogation.

In the spring of 1988, I met the priest Jorge Osorio in Uruguay. He is a member of the nonviolence group Serpaj, and during the dictatorship he participated in civil disobedience activities. He shared several interesting experiences with me. His group had, for example, decided which subject each activist would talk about during the interrogation. One was to talk about Serpaj, another was to provide facts about oppression, another would be responsible for the legal aspects, and Jorge would answer questions about political prisoners. With this system they could prepare themselves well. If the questions dealt with other topics, Jorge referred them to other members of the group.

When other people can seriously be endangered you should sometimes choose not to participate in the interrogation at all, or restrict your answers to only a few questions, such as your name and address. On a field trip to Israel, all the Swedish participants were stopped by the police. They were interrogated about which Palestinians they had visited, and without thinking provided the names. This obedience was even more incomprehensible when it became apparent that the Swedes were political members of the solidarity movement. Obedience, however, seems to be something we all have in common in Europe, independent of political affiliation or involvement. A standard phrase is effective in getting us to talk: "You must answer the question."

Peter Wright, who for more than twenty years worked for the British security agency, writes in his memoirs about their interrogation methods.[39] The secret is that the interrogator must gain the advantage over the person being interrogated. Interrogators can do this by presenting facts and implying that they know everything, and that the interrogation is really just a formality: "I just want to know your opinion about what your friend just told us."

It is more common, however, to ask different questions about the same thing. Then it is possible to get the person being interrogated to contradict him- or herself. By confronting the victim with his or her own lies, resistance is broken down. This method is most effective if it is used over and over again at repeated interrogations. This method has been used successfully by police in interrogations of refugees, according to an interpreter I interviewed for a study that I was doing. He interpreted at police interrogations of people applying for asylum. If the interrogator is systematic and precise, it becomes relatively easy to find deviations, inaccuracies, or omissions.

A story can also be judged according to its structure. When people being interrogated provide irrelevant details, this strengthens their credibility. A liar has no reason to add unnecessary made-up details that would be difficult to remember at later interrogations. Even being uncertain about details can indicate that a testimony is true.

Another way of judging evidence is to analyze the tendencies in the answers. In what way is the person being interrogated biased? Nonviolence activists often break this one-sided tendency by discussing things from different points of view. The two most well-known nonviolence trainers in the world, Hildegard Goss-Mayr and Jean Goss, emphasized the importance of reasoning from the opponent's point of view.

When interrogators put together the information they have obtained, they often know more than the interrogated person can predict. A Swedish peace activist was arrested in possession of a map of a military air base outside of Oslo, Norway, that we suspected was used for airplanes armed with nuclear weapons. Together with someone else, I had worked for three days on improving the map only the week before.

Based on our two handwritings, the police suspected two things: either two people had copied another map or they had been at the air base. They simply asked the peace activist if someone had been at the air base before him. He confirmed that people had been there, but did not want to provide any names. But the police had also found an address list that had been sent around in our affinity group. We had filled in the list with our own handwriting. His answer was sufficient to give the police evidence that the two of us had been there.

He also happened to mention that he had eaten at a certain restaurant, which interested the police very much. When the activist asked why, the police answered that they could interrogate the employees of the restaurant. Since several of us met at that restaurant, the police could gain information about which of us had been there. They had an address list and could show our passport photographs to the restaurant employees. None of this information was secret, and each of us could have called the police and informed them that we were involved. It would, however, have been more serious if the information had been about people that were not prepared to be tried in a court of law.

In my book *Plowshares Number 8*, I describe two interrogation "tricks."[40] These were tried on the members of my own group, Pershing Plowshares, by an agent from Florida's Metropolitan Bureau of Investigation. Since I have already described these attempts in my other book, I am not going to reveal here whether he was successful or not.... The first interrogation trick was an attempt to expose a possible conspiracy. He asked if we had heard his name before. Since he had been an infiltrator in a local peace group, we should have known about him if we cooperated with that group. By finding out if you know certain information, the interrogator can find out which people or groups help you or give you information. The second trick was an attempt to lead us into a trap. By asking us if we cooperated with preposterous groups, he tried to get us to start answering. When he then suddenly began asking relevant questions, he would be able to guess the answers if we suddenly refused to answer.

But the problem is seldom that you happen to say too much. During long telephone conversations and in court proceedings, I have tried to supplement incomplete interrogation minutes. Often, the interrogation can be quite rewarding. The police frequently appreciate good discussions just like anybody else. Why not ask if you can buy them a cup of coffee from the coffee machine in the hall?

There is a danger in taking on stereotypical roles. Why should you wait for questions before you start telling your story? And who says that only one side should ask the questions?

Prison Solidarity

One hundred thousand dollars! That is how much each and every one of us would have to pay to be released on bail after our Plowshares action in Florida. Then suddenly the sum was reduced to zero. The police tried to scare us at first. When the international support grew too strong, they wanted to get rid of us as soon as possible.

There was one exception—Patrick O'Neill had broken a conditional sentence that he had had from a previous action. His bail was set at ten thousand dollars. As soon as the judge reduced the bail for me, representatives of the court came to my cell. They wanted me to sign a paper that promised that I would appear at the trial. I refused because they would not release Patrick. Some people thought it was strange that I voluntarily remained in jail. But *prison solidarity* increases the moral pressure on the authorities. After two months they removed Patrick's bail requirement and we could leave the jail together.

One aim of prison solidarity can be that everybody be released at the same time. This tactic is often used directly after being arrested if there is a risk that somebody will not be released together with the others. In solidarity with those that risk being detained, everybody refuses to cooperate until they are released.

On a rainy day in October 1983, four hundred people were closed in a kennel-like area on Griffiss Air Force Base in New York State. Many people became chilled, either because they were sick or because they were not properly dressed. The situation was pretty serious. Some people started sending messages from cage to cage: we needed to decide what to do. We soon made up our minds that about one hundred of us would stay until those that were in the greatest need were allowed inside or released. But suddenly, the military commander became angry. He gave the order that all of us should be carried in. Inside the cells, the solidarity action was continued by some people who refused to cooperate with the interrogation until the others were released.

Prison solidarity can also be used in certain situations for the sake of principles. When the police are violent, many people refuse to obey orders or to cooperate with the interrogations. A friend from Argentina, Amanda Peralta, refused to cooperate with interrogators as long as a particular military officer was present. He had previously tortured her. When the police threw the officer out he went crazy with fury.

COMMUNICATION

Stellan politely thanks the German police for the interesting acquaintanceship made during his time under arrest. With mixed feelings, he leaves the prison. Why did his affinity group pay his bail? What was happening out there? It must be something serious. Ylva and Johanna find him at the entrance. They are worried and embrace him. What had happened in prison? Why had he asked to be released?

This incident was preceded by the district attorney's calling the support group directly and asking them to pay Stellan Vinthagen's bail. A very strange thing to do, you might think. To increase the moral pressure on the authorities, Stellan had decided not to leave jail after his Plowshares action in Mutlangen. When the district attorney didn't succeed in convincing the support group, the police contacted them: "He is crying desperately in his cell. He is begging to be allowed out. The guy just can't deal with the life of a prisoner." Quickly the support group collects the two thousand German marks and pays the bail.

It isn't until Ylva and Johanna drive Stellan home that they realize that the police have fooled them. Stellan was completely set on staying in jail. The group's mistake was that they did not decide beforehand how they would communicate after the arrest. Similar problems arise at most actions. Affinity groups forget to prepare themselves for the communication difficulties that almost always arise when doing civil disobedience.

Before the action, the people that the action is directed against should be contacted if possible. To avoid an ever increasing resistance, an environmentally destructive company may want to negotiate a solution, for example. Usually, the police are contacted so that they have the time they need to prepare themselves. As I mentioned before, this reduces the risk of their being nervous. Affinity groups can also reach some practical agreements with the police about how the action should be done.

One group that is often overlooked are the workers that can be affected by the action. These people probably also have opinions that the affinity group should take into consideration. Nonchalance from the activists can cause unnecessary tensions. In several cases, negotiations with workers have led to support actions or agreements that they will not work during the action.

The different peacekeepers can divide the responsibility between them to maintain contact with the police and the workers. An arrest is usually preceded by a period of time when the police have to wait around. The goal of the peacekeepers can be to make personal contact with every police officer during this time.

The affinity group is usually confined to a certain place. The *contact people* give them the possibility of communicating and making new decisions. It is even more difficult to make decisions after being arrested. The affinity group can decide either to not make any decisions before everybody has contact with each other, or to delegate the right to make decisions to a few people. When I participated in a Plowshares action in 1984, we were arrested and placed in the Orlando County Jail. But we were split up in different cells and prison buildings. Nobody in our support group had the right to visit us. Our messages to each other were delivered first by a lawyer and then by a Catholic priest.

After the action, you also need to communicate with other activists, the opponent, and others. When Gunilla Åkerberg and Anders Grip did their Plowshares action in Kristinehamn, Sweden, in February 1989, a mailing was sent out all over the world. This led to a support statement from a peace group in Thailand and from the nonviolence movement Serpaj, which consists of hundreds of local and national groups all over Latin America.

Media

This handbook is a kind of medium. It communicates some thoughts about and experiences in civil disobedience. Before I take up more practical problems with the mass media, I would like to lay out an interesting discussion about the role of the official media in society. This discussion has changed my conceptions entirely.

The democratic goal of civil disobedience is to achieve a broad participation in the decisionmaking process, or, in other words, to create dialogue and cooperation. Democracy has been realized when all those concerned are involved in a discussion that leads to good decisions for everyone, i.e., agreements. If some people are ignored, then they can use civil disobedience to get the democratic process going again.

Other ways exist of looking at civil disobedience. Actions can be aimed at directly influencing those in control. Not to have to get a dialogue going can certainly be more effective. But in the long run, these actions undermine democracy. Of course, the same problem arises when those who have the power make what they think are good decisions without discussing them beforehand with the people involved.

Not all the people involved have to participate in the dialogue. But everybody should have a fair chance to do so if they want to. By dialogue I mean direct conversation between people. In the debates staged in the mass media, only a limited number of the people participate. You do not participate in a dialogue just by reading a text. A text does not answer when addressed. Not even when you follow a series of debate articles in the newspaper does the text begin to answer or reflect over what you think about it. It is unchangeable. A text is static from the moment it is printed.

The understanding of a text, however, is not static. It can be developed during a debate about the contents of the text. The text becomes general property when it is printed. Not even the author has a privileged right to interpret a written text; if an author writes a new debate article for the newspaper a week later with new, more subtle opinions, it is just a new text. The old debate article still exists and has not been changed at all. A conversation can be about a text. The text can add something important to the conversation. The written word cannot, however, be confused with a dialogue.

Today, the expression "public debate" is often used to describe what is presented in the mass media. This is misleading. Since democracy is based on public debate, this new meaning becomes dangerous. Democracy becomes distorted. The fact that suggestions, viewpoints, and information are made public by the mass media is necessary and a good thing for democracy, but publishing provides only the background for the public *debate* that goes on between people. Publicity without discussion is merely entertainment for the public. It becomes a compensation for democracy, and controls the citizens instead. With public debate there is no audience—only participants.

Therefore, it is also misleading to criticize the mass media because they do not provide enough space for public debate, or because they are not effective in representing this debate. Though such criticism can be intended to uphold democracy, in reality it takes power away from the public by taking the function that democracy is founded on—public debate—away from the citizens. Publicity without a public *debate* can cause people to buy particular products or to choose certain people or parties in political elections. Above all, it can make us more passive. Civil disobedience that is covered by the press makes us sigh thankfully: "Isn't it great that somebody is doing something!"

The public media did not always pacify us. Earlier, during the bourgeois revolution, it was a *tool* for democratic debate. The social philosopher Jürgen Habermas, in an early work from 1962, showed how the public destroyed the power of the totalitarian state.[41] He also showed how "the public" has been falling apart since the nineteenth century, with political debate becoming an unpolitical consumption of mass culture.

In coffee shops and parlors an ongoing public debate was developed during the 1700s and 1800s. Newspapers and books were read at home in private, but they were discussed in public. The monopoly on interpretation that belonged to the church and state authorities was often criticized. Through these debates a public opinion was developed, which was seen as an expression of what was true and just. The so-called physiocrats, one of the early bourgeois movements, derived the law from the *common sense* that was the *result* of the public debate. An accepted prerequisite for the development of common sense was that all participants had to be equal and independent, and so this was guaranteed by the fact that these discussions took place mainly between property owners. They did not serve anybody else's interests but their own.

In spite of the fact that this early tradition excluded large groups of people—women, for example—this bourgeois project had strong democratic tendencies. In French cafés, poor women are said to have read newspapers aloud for each other, not having the money, of course, to buy their own copies. In this way, they also developed the public debate.

Habermas uses Kant to further his argument. During the early Enlightenment of the 1700s, Immanuel Kant stated that someone who has been legally declared incompetent "is unable to make up his mind without the leadership of someone else." However, according to Kant, enlightenment is thinking aloud: "how well we would think if we thought, so to speak, together with others."[42] When people who had no source of income other than their own labor started to penetrate the public arena during the 1800s, the liberals were shocked by the strength of their ideas. But the search for the true and just decision was replaced by a division of power. John Stuart Mill and others started to see public opinion as one power among other powers. Later, decisions were made by compromise between different interest groups rather than by debate among the citizens. Democracy was replaced by a division of power. Public debate lost its political characteristic and since then has had a consuming function rather than a reasoning one.

A perfect example of the public as consumers is the panel debates in the grassroots movements, where the discussion is really entertainment. The activist that goes on speech tours becomes a performer. The result is pacification, rather than a dialogue that leads to decisions on appropriate action. Speeches, panel debates, films, slide shows, or books are not very effective if they are not used together with small group discussions. But if they become *tools* for a conversation, they can function as democratic, political measures.

For civil disobedience to function democratically, there must be physical space—places—where the public debate about what is right and just can take place. Discussions with friends and family are probably the most effective media for civil disobedience. Other channels that can be used to increase participation are direct contact and discussions with the opponent during actions and trials. Nonviolence training and building new affinity groups can be seen as media to increase resistance.

Unfortunately, the protest movement is often looking more for publicity than for publicizing. People try to affect the decisionmaking process rather than concentrating on bringing forth problems that need to be discussed. The main issue has become how to get in contact with the mass media and thereby strengthen one's own prestige. Instead of practicing politics through a public debate, people choose to participate in public manifestations and demonstrations. Those who at first really were working for democracy now manipulate the public opinion instead.

The parlors and coffee houses disappeared a long time ago. Politics today should be about how to replace them.

Contact with the Mass Media

"We don't want information from you people. Don't call us again!"

"We just had an editorial staff meeting and we decided that we are not going to support terrorist actions."

"It is fantastic that somebody is doing something! Do you have pictures? We'll send a taxi over. I'll call you right back."

"Since you didn't let us be present at the action, we decided not to cover it."

These are the reactions that the press contact person got from the major newspapers and TV news programs in Sweden when he called them up to tell them about the Pershings to Plowshares action in Germany in 1986. Experience from other actions shows that the same newspapers or TV programs that have boycotted civil disobedience in the past can become interested later and present a balanced and factual picture. If a boycott is not a conscious decision, then it probably has to do with the people that happen to be on the editorial news staff at any given time.

Editors have stopped news stories when they felt that the affinity group's press contact person hadn't respected the prevailing hierarchy. It can be perceived as manipulation to contact only journalists without also contacting the editor. Aside from political reasons for boycotting civil disobedience, journalists quickly lose interest if they think that the activists are doing something solely for the sake of getting into the papers. It is very important that civil disobedience never become *mass media actions*. Disobedience must function totally independently of media coverage.

Sometimes, however, journalists can make an action more sensational or *spectacular*. Then the action takes on a ridiculous and superficial appearance. This happened in 1983 when an affinity group planned a memorial service at an arms manufacturer for people killed by those arms. We were inexperienced and let a TV photographer break our circle so that he could film from inside the circle. The solemnity disappeared and the ceremony felt insincere. It is better to get calm coverage than embarrassing, sensational headlines.

In the actions that I have participated in, we have usually established a special group that is responsible for contacts with the press. They send out press packages, write articles, and do interviews. Aside from the press group, you should also choose some people to document the action, with both photographs and film. To go on tour with a slide show, used together with discussion, is often a more effective "mass media" than a few headlines.

The Press Package

A press package is sent to different editors that might be interested in an action. Mailings are often sent only to the editorial news staff, but the debate, culture, religion, and daily living pages shouldn't be forgotten. You can, of course, fax or mail information directly to individual journalists. So that you don't get lost among thousands of other news items, press releases need to be followed up by telephone calls. A press package can be sent out one week before an action, and another could be sent right before the action and another right afterwards.

You usually put the press release on top of the press package. A press release should be about a half a page long. What editor has the time to read a whole page if her or his office is flooded with news stories? Its contents are structured like an upside-down pyramid: the most important things first, and details and explanations come last. One essential fact is the telephone number of a contact person. Once we forgot that. The mailing was then pretty much meaningless and we had to do a new one. It is a good idea if the press release is somewhat personal. But it should be written in an objective style and all opinions should be presented as quotes. Personally, I always have trouble doing this right.

Photos with captions, the names of the people in the photos, and even the photographers' names can be included in the mailing. Photographers have tried to convince me several times that pictures are more important for newspapers than texts.

Statements, fact sheets, and information about the affinity group are included as separate appendices. The journalist who decides to cover the story might want more background information than only what is covered in the press release.

Interviews

"What gives you the right to do a violent action?" the TV reporter asked as the TV camera zoomed accusingly in on Todd Kaplan.

Todd thought that he found himself in a dialogue. So he started to explain our symbols. "The simple tools that we use show that the action was creative and was therefore not an act of violence. Quite the opposite, the action was based on nonviolence." Radio and TV often cut out the end of what you say. It is important to address any allusions or statements contained in the question first. To the viewer it seemed that Todd defended violence by saying that the symbols were creative.

Even in newspapers, activists can seem to confirm incorrect statements made by journalists:

"Are you disappointed that not that many people showed up?"

"Are you critical of people who use democratic methods?"

"How do you answer all the criticism that you have gotten from the public?"

"Are militant methods more effective than political work?"

Interviews are usually not this biased. Most of the journalists I have met are trying to do a good job. The fact that I almost always find some factual error when I read their articles later is more due to the journalists' lack of time than to ill will.

In order to reduce the risk that an article get written in a biased way, here are some tips on how to deal with the mass media:

- Rotate the people who are interviewed.
- Make sure that the gender division is somewhat even. Otherwise, certain issues are easily perceived as being male, like the draft, or female, like pornography.
- Don't answer questions that are gender discriminatory, irrelevant to the work of the group, or about your private life.
- Avoid making statements for others if nothing has been agreed upon beforehand. Let everybody speak for her- or himself. Even the people who are not present at the interview have this right. If a journalist wants to quote someone, then it is appropriate that the person in question is contacted.
- Find out if it is possible to read the article before it is published.
- Evaluate the article in written form and send the evaluation to the affinity group's list of media contacts.

- Boycott the media and journalists that have spread disinformation before. Send out information to other groups and organizations, so they can avoid the same mistakes.

At a course in civil disobedience for a women's group that did actions against pornography shops, one of the participants described an interesting kind of boycott. She is a member of a leftist party. In connection with several of the women's group actions, she contacted the party's newspaper. Clearly, the editorial staff did not think that the actions were "socialist" enough to cover, since they never made it into the paper. Later, at a big and important action at a pornography shop, she just didn't bother to contact the newspaper at all. The large daily papers covered the action well. Suddenly an editor from the party newspaper called and wondered why they had not been informed about the action. The activist explained why. After that, the newspaper boycott was called off.

One problem that is hard to avoid is when ambitious journalists prepare themselves by reading old articles. The people who are interviewed should also *study* these articles in order to correct earlier inaccuracies. I have seen strange information turn up now and again over a period of several years.

CHAPTER V

THE DIALOGUE OF RESISTANCE: ABOUT THE TRIAL

MEETING FACE TO FACE

When I was traveling from Buenos Aires to Montevideo, I made the mistake of taking a hydrofoil. Seasick and shut up in the passenger's cabin on the jolting boat, I happened to sit next to a talkative activist from the West Coast of the U.S. I succeeded in keeping my breakfast down and even managed to listen to some of his engaging stories. He talked about different actions, mostly against the White Trains loaded with arms. At one point I interrupted him and asked why they did all those actions. The answer was quite interesting: "To get a trial!" By being continuously taken to court, his group managed to keep a dialogue going with the decisionmakers.

In the U.S. and Germany this process has led to judges actually acquitting people who engage in civil disobedience. Judge Myron Bright was in charge of an appeal for two Plowshares actions against nuclear weapons silos in Missouri—Plowshares No. 12 and Silo Pruning Hooks. He wrote the following comment: "We have to understand that civil disobedience in different forms, used without violence against other people, is a part of our society. And what is morally correct in the political demonstrator's outlook has changed and improved our society."

Even the prosecution has sometimes supported the defendant. At a bizarre Plowshares trial during the summer of 1985, the judge became so angry at the prosecution, who obviously supported the activists, that he also took over the prosecution's responsibilities in addition to acting as judge.

Hopefully, in the long run such support creates cooperation. In Germany, for example, several judges have become involved in the peace movement. This involvement led to the arrest of fourteen West German judges and prosecutors for *doing* civil disobedience against nuclear weapons during the winter of 1987. When cooperation is eventually established, it means a change in the law and the behavior of the authorities.

The trial is a dialogue with the government, represented by the prosecution, and with the law, represented by the judge. Often it is also a dialogue with representatives of private ownership interests, in the guise of the plaintiff. It can also be a discussion with the workers and the civil servants that are affected by the action, if they are called in as witnesses.

The trial is a survey of facts and arguments for and against. It can therefore be used by the spectators and others as a basis for discussion and for taking a stand on the actions of the people involved. The trial has a symbolic value and functions as a medium for further public discussion as well.

A German peace activist, Uwe Painke, worked full time for a few years in the mid-1980s with the Campaign for Civil Disobedience and Disarmament. He thought that trials were the most important method of activating new people. The people in this campaign who were on trial sent written invitations to relatives and friends. One priest invited his whole congregation. These spectators often became so affected by the trials that they immediately signed the campaign's written promise to do civil disobedience against the Pershing II missiles.

The courtroom is a place where information that is otherwise kept out of the public debate can be brought forth by both the defense and the prosecution. During Plowshares trials, we usually ask the workers that the prosecution has called as witnesses to talk about what they manufacture.

The trial provides other opportunities as well. Depending on what you want to do with it, it is possible to choose between at least four different ways of defending yourself:

- Play down the action to reduce the punishment.
- Defend yourself with other laws. The action was legal because you followed *international* law or *national* law, such as the necessity of self-defense. You can also maintain that you followed *common human* laws, such as natural law, public law, or other moral laws that are a part of our cultural tradition. One example is the fifth commandment: You shall not kill!
- Present an ethical defense. You can argue according to what is right and humane. You can then maintain that these rights are higher than the law, or that human life is more important than the law.
- Turn the trial around: accuse the opponent instead of defending yourself.

Most Plowshares trials are a mixture of the latter three forms of defense. The basic motivation, however, is always to get a discussion going on what is the truth. We discuss the law, using the language of the court, in order to make ourselves better understood. Then we can refer to common moral values. The dialogue during the trial is hardly ever about defending yourself. Rather, we accuse the opponent of acting wrongly.

Refusal to cooperate is sometimes used at the same time as these methods of defense. Democracy assumes that you want to get a public debate going. Of course, you do not have to carry on a discussion based on terms set by the opponent. If the opponent stops certain parts of the discussion, then you can answer with silence. Silence here expresses the desire to get the conversation going again. It also symbolizes the opponent's attempt to stop the democratic discussion. Silence is therefore an important part of the dialogue.

At the trial in Orlando, when I tried to talk about Europe and the fact that Europeans are the intended victims of the Pershing II missiles, the judge stopped me. I then had a minute of silence for today's victims of the arms race—the poor. During the rest of the trial, I chose to be silent. When Elmer Maas, who participated in the first Plowshares action in Pennsylvania in 1980, was not allowed to defend himself at the trial, everybody—including the spectators—turned their backs on the judge. In some cases, people have continued the trial outside of the courthouse.

Before the trial, the affinity group must decide whether to hire a lawyer or not. Lawyers' professional ethics usually make them feel responsible for defending their clients. The responsibility of the defense lawyer is to determine whether the prosecution has presented tenable evidence or not. If the prosecution succeeds in doing so, then the lawyer is responsible for seeing to it that the punishment is as mild as possible. In practice, this can mean that the goals of the lawyer can be in direct opposition to the interests of the affinity group, which are to turn the trial around and to try to discuss the possibilities of resistance. Because of this, activists usually choose to defend themselves. The intent is to get a dialogue going, not to be defended. Of course, when needed, a lawyer can function as an adviser.

The Different Phases of the Trial

A trial can be divided into five parts: presentation of the plaintiff's case, description of the crime, presentation of the evidence, discussions about responsibility, and sentencing. The prosecution presents its case, which covers the charges. Then the defendant has the opportunity to admit to being guilty. Then you can either admit to or deny having broken the law.

"I have not broken the law with my action, but I admit to having committed crimes against the poor by not stopping arms export." That is how I answered the charges against me at a trial after an action against arms export. After doing civil disobedience, activists often admit to breaking the law but maintain that it was necessary under the circumstances.

The next important part of the trial is when the prosecution and the defense each give their versions of the series of events in question. If the prosecution takes up irrelevant or misleading questions, you can protest. You are also given the opportunity to ask the prosecutor's witnesses questions. This gives you the possibility of starting a moral discussion. By asking concrete questions you can get them to describe the opponent's activities.

After the prosecution, it is the defendant's turn to describe what has happened, with the help of witnesses. This presentation can include information about your personal background, important events and people in your life, how the action was planned, and what inspired you to do the action. The latter can be an account of international laws that you intended to follow, for example. With slides or by demonstrating and explaining the chain of events, the action can be dramatized. Don't forget to submit evidence, such as banners and symbols. It is usually possible to read statements. Some people have even been allowed to sing the songs that were sung during the action!

Witnesses can describe what happened. Employees can talk about what happens inside a company. Friends can testify about the personality of the accused or describe earlier "crimes." Experts can provide specific information about international law or the situation in the Third World, for instance. The prosecution usually asks both the accused and their witnesses questions. These questions provide additional opportunities to turn prejudices around or correct inaccurate notions.

After this presentation of the background and the series of events, both the prosecution and the defense are given the opportunity to evaluate the action and discuss the question of responsibility. This is the point when it is especially important to emphasize the intent of the action: what you wanted to achieve, what civil disobedience and nonviolence means, what is right and wrong, and who is responsible.

You should probably provide some suggestions for what the trial should lead to. This plea can be about the punishment. But it is just as important to discuss what the judge, the prosecutor, and the citizens can do to stop the unjust, criminal acts that the trial is really about.

It is problematic to ask for a mild punishment. Then you maintain that you should be punished and therefore have done wrong. I usually ask to be declared not guilty. If I have done something wrong, I should really get the *hardest* punishment since I have repeatedly broken the law. In addition, the actions were well planned and organized, without extenuating circumstances like "spontaneous reactions." Not only that, I challenge and agitate others to continue the resistance. This does not mean that I believe in punishment. But as long as others are punished, I do not think that I should get any special treatment.

If the trial leads to acquittal, then the action has been approved by the court. This can provide support for others to continue. The development of the right to freedom of speech is an example of this kind of recognition. If you are found guilty, the punishment becomes a challenge for others to continue the resistance. An appeal means a continuation of the dialogue. It isn't uncommon to be acquitted after an appeal. A higher court can provide a greater opportunity to discuss questions of principle.

CHAPTER VI

POWER OF RESISTANCE:
ABOUT PUNISHMENT

OVERCOMING FEAR

The punishment is the most important part of civil disobedience. The exception is being declared not guilty when the law in principle accepts the action. The fear of personal consequences often prevents us from stopping violence and creating a more just society. The means of breaking this paralysis, paradoxically enough, is to take the consequences of disobedience—to take the punishment.

When people do resistance against injustice even though it may lead to dismissal, slander, restitution, or imprisonment, the punishment is nullified. Or, to express it more clearly: the main function of the punishment, to make citizens internalize control—so that they become their own jailers—loses its effect.

A prison is designed above all for the people that are *not* inside it. When citizens do what they perceive as the right thing, independently of the risk of punishment, then the walls are torn down. Physically, the prison is still there. The prisoners that are locked up in it—as a symbolic hint to the rest of us—are still there. But the primary prisoners—the people outside of the walls—free themselves from their chains through disobedience.

The real chains are the fears of the personal consequences of breaking the law or conventions. This fear is not only psychological. The chains are above all a social and cultural creation. The construction of these chains can vary. In the Scandinavian countries, we build up our imprisonment based on anxiety about what might happen with work or school, what our friends are going to say, how we are going to fulfill our duties to our families, and what kind of problems restitution can cause.

When a Swedish group planned a Plowshares action, we discovered that economic consequences are more serious obstacles for resistance than prison. During the preparations we spent a few hours talking about our feelings about going to jail. Nobody seemed especially worried about imprisonment. Later, however, it became apparent that just about everybody was restrained by their fear of having to pay restitution. Several people were thinking about avoiding paying damages by giving their capital resources to their siblings or spouses.

In another group, with somewhat younger participants—around thirty years old—the fear of having to pay restitution for the damages was not as strong. This group consisted of "alternative" people who lived in collectives or in the countryside. In spite of the fact that they were less established than the teachers, doctors, and civil servants in the first group, they were more anxious about what would happen with their jobs or educations. Sometimes they did not dare to take time off work or miss a lecture:

"My substitute probably won't like my changing my work schedule again."

"My colleagues are starting to sneer at me."

"No, I can't do that. I have to present a paper."

It isn't the height of the walls that stops the prisoners from escaping. It isn't the degree of punishment that makes us start controlling ourselves. It is our *attitude* toward punishment that decides its effectiveness. A functioning control does not have to threaten us with very much. We often assign a mystical significance to the threat of punishment. One of the strongest chains on us today is the idea of that horrible *black mark*. Thus, some social workers do not pay support to refugees that are in hiding, because it can mean a black mark on their record.

The punishment can come from different directions. It may come from the side, from friends, for instance. It can even come from below. Perhaps you will no longer be able to narcissistically confirm your self-confidence through other people's admiration and respect. I am afraid of being misunderstood, for instance. I hate being laughed at. I don't want people to think that I am trying to act superior. Long prison sentences or a persistent federal marshal cause me to have serious apprehensions. All of this and a lot of other things make me want to be obedient, though also a critical and revealing author that peacefully demonstrates a few times a year. The fear is there all the time. I can't avoid it. But I can overcome it. And if I can overcome it, my prison is nullified.

Since fear is the final obstacle for us in creating a more just society, punishment is the most important part of civil disobedience. As long as there is fear, there must be people who challenge the threat of punishment; otherwise, the fear will control us. Henry David Thoreau expressed this principle for effective civil disobedience as early as 1849:

> Under a government which imprisons any unjustly, the true place for a just man is also in prison. The proper place today, the only place which Massachusetts has provided for her freer and less desponding spirits, is in her prisons.... [It is] the only house in a slave State in which a

free man can abide with honor. If any think that their influence would be lost there, and their voices no longer afflict the ear of the State, that they would not be as an enemy within its walls, they do not know by how much truth is stronger than error, nor how much more eloquently and effectively he can combat injustice who has experienced a little in his own person.[43]

Even Gandhi saw personal consequences as the strength behind civil disobedience. A satyagrahi believes that "meek suffering for a just cause has a virtue all its own and is infinitely greater than the virtue of the sword."[44]

Civil disobedience does not, however, mean martyrdom. It isn't suffering that creates strength. Many people get by just fine in prison. The strength of civil disobedience lies in *overcoming the fear* of suffering. The whole challenge is in overcoming fear. It forces us to realize what our possibilities are. Martyrs do exactly the opposite. They take opportunities away from others. We love them because they offer themselves for us. They are our proxies. But nobody else can free us. Freedom can be won only by overcoming fear and taking the consequences. To do the opposite, to try to escape from punishment and be disobedient in secret, is to confirm obedience. Running away strengthens the effect of the punishment.

When two switch-tenders told the conductor, Lars Falkenberg, that he was to drive a train loaded with arms that night, he had the alternative of calling in sick. He could have avoided a conflict with his employer and the judicial system. It would have been a private, moral action that might have given Lars a clear conscience. On the other hand, it would have strengthened the other drivers' conviction that refusal, with consequent dismissal, was not an alternative. When Lars refused to drive the train, he demystified the threat of dismissal. In spite of—or maybe because of—the fact that he was fired, his personal risk-taking inspired others to be disobedient.

At Danbury's federal prison in Connecticut, there was a half-official disobedience that the guards did not try to stop. In my cell, we had hidden a hot plate that some mafioso guy past the age of retirement had stolen from the guards' cafeteria. A steady influx of canned octopus and mussels was smuggled in from the outside. Spaghetti, garlic, and grated cheese were stolen from the kitchen. At night the singular scent of Italian pasta spread down the corridors. At first, I was surprised that the guards pretended they didn't notice this going on. A lot went on right under their noses. Later, I understood that our sneaking around meant that we were controlling ourselves. It was very unusual for us to seriously protest against something or do resistance in the face of an unjust situation, because then we risked the guards' cracking down on our undercover operations.

When I visited a slum in Santiago, I often saw thin wires connected to the street lamps, which meant stolen electricity. While this theft was of course morally defensible since the electricity allowed poor people to survive cold winter nights, at the same time it prevented them from doing something that would get the attention of the authorities. It stopped them from getting organized and demanding a functional and inexpensive energy supply. Their possibilities were in a locked position.

Not even the most harsh dictator states have the resources to hire enough police to control each and every person. The citizens have to control themselves and each other. Prince Kropotkin maintained that development arises from mutual help. I would add that power is developed based on mutual control. In order for punishment to have any effect we have to keep ourselves under control. The idea of civil disobedience is to break this self-control and publicly challenge others to overcome it. The goal is to create a culture where citizens stop injustice and violence directly, without allowing themselves to be hindered by threats of punishment.

The Opportunities Provided by Punishment

Civil disobedience has sometimes been criticized for being a waste of time. You can do so much when you have your freedom. The money that you have to pay the marshal for restitution could be sent to the Third World. When you get fired, you lose your ability to influence your place of work. If I do something too extreme, then I lose the confidence of others.

This is based on a misunderstanding. The assumption that punishment is an unfortunate consequence of resistance is incorrect. Punishment is the source of the strength of civil disobedience. This strength is needed for resistance to bear new fruit. People who stand tall in the face of slander break the power of slander. People who stand tall but lower their heads in order to try to escape their neighbors' derision confirm the power of derision.

Two exceptions exist to the necessity of punishment. When the nonviolence movement is strong enough to achieve its goals with its own strength, then punishment is not needed. Neither is it needed if you are close to an agreement with the opponent. The occupation to protect the Kynne Hills from exploratory drilling, which I mentioned earlier, is an example of the first exception. Such a large part of the population participated, and their constant readiness was so morally strong, that the authorities never dared to devastate the hills. Actions in Stockholm and Gothenburg during the 1970s to save old trees and buildings from being destroyed are examples of the other exception. During these occupations, enough politicians came out in support that the trees were saved in both cities.

Another time when punishment is not needed is when you are declared *not guilty*. In this case, the law basically takes the side of the resistance against the government. A German judge, for example, suddenly started acquitting people who did actions against the Pershing II base in Mutlangen. In the end, the authorities had to prevent him from judging in civil disobedience cases.

However, opportunities to reach a quick agreement are seldom. It also takes time to build up a resistance that is so morally strong that the opponent avoids defying it. So in most cases civil disobedience is dependent on punishment.

Punishment adds four qualities to the struggle:

- As I mentioned before, it helps to *nullify its own intended power*.
- It gives the message the form of a *moral appeal*, which can create support among people on the opponent's side.
- It functions as a *challenge* to the people who passively support the system to break their pattern of obedience.
- The symbolism that the opponent adds by assigning punishment provides a *holistic understanding* of resistance. Resistance is not a monologue, but a dialogue where the opponent participates and takes a stand.

On a night in December 1955 in Montgomery, Alabama, a tired African-American woman named Rosa Parks sat in the front of the bus, on a seat that was reserved for white people. She refused to give up her seat to a white man and was arrested, thereby refusing punishment its power. This imprisonment led to a 382-day bus boycott, and created a civil rights movement that radically changed the U.S.'s apartheid laws. The movement's endurance of police brutality caused surprisingly strong support among the white middle class. The second function of punishment is just this—the function of moral appeal.

The third function of punishment is to challenge people who passively support the system to break out of their obedience. This works above all with friends, workers, and others that you meet in connection with the action, representatives from the powers that be, and people you meet after being released.

The fourth function of punishment is the opponent's contribution to the struggle. The symbolism that they bring into the discussion by assigning punishment provides a dynamic understanding of resistance. By not putting ourselves above the law and by taking the punishment instead, we create an interplay with the opponent where they become a part of the struggle. The resistance becomes not a demonstration or manifestation, but a dialogue in which the opponent participates and takes a stand.

Punishment and Resistance

Imprisonment provides a steadier political platform than the action or the trial. It is a waste of strength and energy not to plan your imprisonment. Quite a number of books have been written in prison. I wrote most of my first book in prison. I also exchanged letters with people from all over the world, like Zimbabwe, Australia, and Costa Rica. Another Plowshares activist, Martin Holladay, who was in the same prison as I was, chose one country at a time and wrote articles about the Plowshares movement in the papers of that country. Many Plowshares prisoners exchange letters with politicians and judges, soldiers, and workers at arms factories. From a political perspective, I have never been as effective outside of the walls as I have in prison.

Gandhi said that one of the goals of time in prison was to gain the opponent's respect.[45] He gave six guidelines for an imprisoned satyagrahi:

- Be honest.
- Cooperate with the prison administration.
- Set an example for other prisoners by your obedience.
- Never ask for privileges that the lowest fellow prisoner does not have and that are not needed strictly for health reasons.
- Do not fail to ask for what you do need and do not become irritated if you do not get it.
- Do everything that is asked of you as well as possible.

Gandhi maintained that this kind of behavior in prison would make the position of the government unsustainable. Sometimes, however, you have to do resistance in prison, such as when the guards break the prison regulations and treat you without respect. Several political prisoners have criticized Gandhi and emphasized other occasions where you should do resistance in connection with punishment. During the 1980s, this kind of action became quite common.

Other historic examples of prison resistance exist as well. On August 11, 1943, nineteen draft refusers started a six-month strike in Danbury's Federal Correctional Institution as a protest against racial segregation in the cafeteria. I was locked up in the same worn-out prison forty-one years later. The prison had by that time earned an illustrious reputation for resistance. During the Vietnam War, the priest and Plowshares activist Phil Berrigan organized a strike there in which most of the prisoners participated. Right before I was sent there, a peace activist had done an action against the prison's cable factory, where prisoners made cables for nuclear weapons and space shuttles.

The intent of actions during imprisonment can be to continue the resistance for which you were locked up. One of the most interesting examples is Corbett Bishop, a draft resister during World War II. He was arrested on September 9, 1944. He told the police that the spirit is free and if they wanted his body they would have to take it without his cooperation. He refused to eat, stand up, or dress himself. He was force-fed and carried around in the prison and the court. After 144 days, he was suddenly released on probation from his four-year sentence. But he refused to cooperate with his probation. He was locked up again to serve the rest of his sentence. After a total of 193 days of noncooperation, he was released without any conditions at all.

Some actions are directed at the prison system itself. Refusal to work as a protest against forced labor is common. I refused to work in the prison industries. I did this because in the first place it was a profitable business for the prison and in the second place they made cables for nuclear weapons there. Many activists also refuse to participate in the prison's control system, such as blood and urine tests, frisking, and psychological tests.

Helen Woodson is serving a seventeen-year prison sentence for a Plowshares action. She addressed both the military's and the prison system's lack of respect for life when she did what she calls an Isaiah 49 action on March 16, 1988.

In the ninth verse, the Lord encourages prisoners to "walk out" and leave imprisonment; Helen did this and explained why in a flyer she gave to the guard. Like most prison actions, her walk-out led to her being put in an isolation cell. This succeeded only in giving the action a stronger symbolic meaning.

Actions are often done for a limited period of time, such as a one-day refusal to obey orders on the anniversary of the bombing of Hiroshima. You can also, because of moral reasons, refuse to participate in certain prison phenomena, including noncooperation with the prison system itself.

It is important that the intents of prison actions be made very clear so that they are not perceived as an escape from punishment. Resistance should be out in the open. If you plan not to show up at the prison when you are called in to serve your sentence, then you could follow the example of the Norwegian activist Morten Rönning. In August 1987, he was to start serving a prison sentence for refusing to pay fines for an action against a military air base outside of Oslo that can receive airplanes armed with nuclear weapons. On the day he was supposed to go to the prison, he participated in a blockade of the airstrip at the air base instead.

Resistance is also common in the case of fines and restitution. In the Plowshares movement we usually refuse to pay for the disarmament we carry out, since the money would be used to repair the weapons. When you refuse to pay fines or damages, the court sends your case on to the marshal. Sometimes this transfer provides new opportunities for creative resistance. The German marshals have tried unsuccessfully several times to collect from the peace activist Uwe Painke, for instance. He agrees to meet them at public places, like in churches during services or in student cafeterias during lunch. On one occasion he invited his friends and representatives from the media over to his house when he knew that the marshals were on the way over. The marshals have refused several times to do their job "under such circumstances."

Several problems with resistance in connection with both imprisonment and fines make people choose to do it only in certain circumstances. In the Pershing Plowshares action group in Florida, we were afraid of losing the *focus* of the resistance. The message of our action could become diffuse if we did new actions about all kinds of issues during imprisonment. In addition, we would probably not have enough energy to continue the work necessary around the action, and we might lose concentration. So that resistance in connection with punishment does not obscure the struggle, our actions should be constructive and show the goodwill of the participants. For example, when workers are fired for conscientious objection they can do a *reverse strike* by continuing to work in spite of being fired.

Since fines prevent many people from participating in civil disobedience, you can make a point by paying them. If fines are never paid, then people's feeling that fines are something that you should avoid at all costs can be intensified. Restitution is somewhat more problematic, since the money goes directly to that which we are struggling against. It is possible to do what the Plowshares activist Anders Grip did. After disarming a weapon that was about to be exported, he offered to pay restitution to people who had been subjected to the Swedish weapons that he had not succeeded in disarming.

Another problem that many Plowshares groups in the U.S. are forced to take into consideration is how to actually carry out prison resistance. With our relatively long sentences—my group got three years in prison and five years on probation—a continued resistance could have meant up to eight years in isolation. Since we severely limited our resistance to just a few issues, we were released after one to two years, with only short periods of time in isolation. Those who do civil disobedience are not superhuman. Being human means making compromises.

Coping with Imprisonment

When the Plowshares activist Helen Woodson had served one-third of her eighteen-year sentence, I wrote her a letter, telling her about the handbook in civil disobedience that I had started to write. I asked her for help. My question was: How can you deal with a long prison sentence? Her answer astounded me:

I am probably not the right person to answer your question. I don't experience prison as difficult. We have to make a lot of decisions in our lives that mean sacrificing our freedom to do other things. Getting married or having children are two examples. Just like resistance, these choices are often about the future and the protection of life. The difference is that these sacrifices are a part of our culture. In our consciousness they are self-evident parts of our lives. If the preservation of life on earth demands resistance, and if resistance means imprisonment, then we should also see this as a part of our lives.

Helen is unique. She likes being in prison.

It is easier to identify with her co-activist, the priest Paul Kabat. He felt that he was dragged to the action against his will, kicking and screaming. His conscience forced him to destroy the lid of a nuclear weapons silo in spite of his fear of the consequences. Paul hated prison. He begged the judge to let him out. After a couple of years the judge obliged him.

I had bad stomachaches the first few days in jail. I didn't know if they were going to deport me, or if I would have to sit for twenty years in a narrow cell. In order not to break down, I sat on the bed and concentrated on my breathing. A Buddhist had given me the idea. I prayed to God frantically to help me calm down. The incomprehensible "medieval" Bible whose translation was commissioned by King James did not provide any comfort whatsoever.

But pretty soon I got used to imprisonment. Sometimes I got on really well. Martin Holladay, from the twelfth Plowshares action, was sent to my prison during the last month before I was released. This was a wonderful time for me and I didn't experience the psychological ordeal that the prisoners called being "short." The end of the jail sentence is generally considered the worst. You get nervous and irritable.

Some people lose control and do something to make sure that they can stay in prison, safe and secure.

After just a couple of months of prison life, the "outside" becomes unreal. The sense of security you feel in prison is partly caused by the pronounced rational daily existence there. The outer frame of life is always determined by privileges and punishment. When you are released, you lose the security of the prison. The feeling is schizophrenic, because at the same time what you want more than anything else is to get out. The pleasant freedom from responsibility also creates a feeling of security. When you have chosen to obey, then there are not so many other choices to be made.

In my book *Plowshares Number 8*, I describe how much it meant to me to move from the top bunk to the lower bunk when it was free.[46] After a couple of months I was moved into a cell with only fifty prisoners instead of ninety. It was like moving away from home for the first time and into my first own apartment, even though I had to sleep on the top bunk again. After six months I had the right once again to the lower bunk. Within the year I was even given my own bed.

The prisoners establish a relationship of dependency with the guards. It is hard to do resistance against someone who gives you an extra blanket during the winter "if you keep quiet 'bout it." If the guards also have the power, when necessary, to give you an extra leave of absence or cancel one, then they can take on characteristics of the early psychoanalysts' caricature of the father figure. The jailer has complete access to freedom. He gets what I desire.

The most difficult thing to realize is the prisoners' control of each other. By an ingenious system of collective punishment the sins of the individual are paid for by the group. When I didn't make my bed wrinkle-free and according to the right measurements, my cellmates had to pay the price.

Sometimes they even made us eat after Block Four, which was no fun. That's where the newcomers were.

The prisoners that defined themselves as political prisoners got by better than the others. There were several reasons for this. We had personal support groups outside of the prison that quickly helped us when we needed them. Many of us also had intellectual interests that we could satisfy better inside prison than outside. I spent several hours a day just discussing. I also plowed through more books during my year in prison than I would have been able to read in three times that time on the outside. Another important difference, implied by Helen Woodson, is that the resister sees prison as a part of the struggle. The thief sees prison as a "damned mistake." The political prisoner is privileged. It is nearly impossible to do anything about that. We have, quite simply, better resources.

It is, however, important to prepare for the time in prison well. What are your rights? And what kind of rights can you demand? What kind of treatment from the guards can you accept? When I was moved to a new prison, I always tried to find out what rules I had to break in order to end up in isolation. If a fellow prisoner became disagreeable then I might have to escape into the "hole."

It is impossible to know beforehand how your time in prison will be. I had not predicted the feeling of frustration at being moved around between prisons. The long periods of waiting in bare cells when I didn't know what would happen or when I would finally get to the real prison were extremely trying. There is no way to prepare yourself for that. Maybe you can practice by waiting in line at the welfare office to see how it feels. But it really isn't the same thing.

CHAPTER VII

A CONDITION FOR RESISTANCE: ABOUT DEMOCRACY

DEVELOPING DEMOCRACY

At the end of the nineteenth century, the liberals and the workers' movement in Europe developed a form of democracy that is used automatically today and sometimes unreflectively passed on. The new democracy was a protest against the political and religious structures of the time, which assigned different values to different people. The society was traditionally seen as a hierarchical organism where various interest groups could affect the course of events to a greater or lesser extent. The grassroots movements developed instead a liberal, atomistic stream of ideas that emphasized the individual and his or her rights. Each and every one of us is just as valuable and we should have the same rights. Nobody's opinion should be worth more than anybody else's.

This new democracy's struggle for the individual was also a struggle for the majority. A minority is not allowed to govern the majority. When the majority of individuals support a suggestion, then their opinion wins. If there are more than two suggestions, then they are voted on in pairs until one of the suggestions wins. The alternative democratic traditions were so weak in Scandinavia that the forms of democracy that grew out of the people's movements were unanimously adopted all over. They quickly became so widely accepted that they were soon perceived as being the ideal forms of democracy that functioned in all situations. This was not the case in the rest of the world. Even if *Robert's Rules of Order*, a classic exposition on majority democracy, was used widely in the Anglo-Saxon world, other kinds of democracy were being developed all the time.

The much more recent tradition that I will describe here has been developed by the movements that have based their work on nonviolence. It attempts to make democracy dynamic and constantly improve and develop it according to changing circumstances. The democratic tools mentioned below are above all from the North American peace and alternative movements. The Philadelphia-based group Movement for a New Society was the one that most systematically developed and published democratic innovations. Several of the democratic tools I describe here were developed by feminist groups.

The 1980s have seen the sharpening of many democratic tools by all kinds of groups, from cooperative companies to pacifist resistance groups. When I lived in the U.S., I was a member of a cooperative bank and a cooperative store. I worked on the editorial staff of a newspaper and did odd jobs at a bakery. In all of these groups we used these new democratic forms. In addition, decisions were made by consensus—agreement—instead of by the majority.

Tools for Democracy

At the end of the sixties, the student movements tried to democratize democracy by simplifying organizations and structures. Large group meetings and informal meetings were popular, but the result was chaotic. During the large group meetings only those that were verbally strong talked. And which decisions were actually made at the "informal" meetings? The interest in *developing* democracy soon cooled off; the unorganized organizations were short-lived. The participants probably got tired of having to always reorganize everything from the beginning whenever something was to be done.

North American feminism and the alternative movements led the development of democracy in the other direction. The old structures were not advanced enough to meet the new demands on democracy. The goal was to find forms that allowed quiet people to be heard and that kept the dominant people in check. The women's movement also wanted to find ways of working that were more effective than the traditional male ways. They believed that the way we work together also determines the results.

The international nonviolence movement enthusiastically took it upon themselves to spread the new ways of working. In the encounter, however, with the old, radical pacifist movements, like India's, for example, these missionaries of democracy discovered that they were not pioneers, at least not in all aspects. The new ideas were often a reawakening of old attempts to create democracy.

I can be pretty skeptical. When I moved to the U.S. and started working in a local peace group in Syracuse, I had heard only rumors about these new forms of democracy. I was difficult to convince. But on the other hand, nobody even tried to convince me. My guard was up at about the first hundred meetings. After a while, I began to see the advantages of the new methods, especially in the context of nonviolence and civil disobedience. Which of these tools are appropriate in other contexts will have to be evaluated by each group.

It was, by the way, the **evaluations** that first got me interested. At the end of each meeting, we had a five-minute evaluation. The point was to emphasize that there was no predefined, necessary form to the meeting. Each group has different needs. Democracy becomes dynamic, changing according to the circumstances and new experiences. During the evaluation, every participant, one after the other, can take up problems that have arisen during the meeting; for example, it felt pressed for time, not everybody had been given the chance to talk, or people interrupted each other. It is important to bring up things that can be improved at the next meeting.

The **round** is a tool that was used by the women's movement early on. The purpose is to inspire everybody to talk and prevent people from dominating. The most common form of round is when you let the person sitting next to you take over and after she is done talking the person next to her takes over, and so on. You can also go in any order you want as long as nobody speaks twice before the round is over. If you don't have anything to say then you can *pass*.

Personal sharing is a tool based on the belief that it is impossible to isolate the meeting from the rest of your life. With the help of a round, we usually talk about how we feel about the meeting and if something special has happened since the last time we met. We usually do personal sharing before we start to discuss the issues at hand. Another expression that some people use to mean about the same thing is *weather report*.

I quickly realized that these personal reports affected the later discussion. A colleague of mine could say, for example, that he felt irritable at the moment because he had watched over his daughter who had the measles all night. Something that often came up was that my colleagues felt worn out because of an excessive work load, or someone had just fallen in love and we had to accept a certain absentmindedness. We had to take these private questions into consideration during heated discussions and when we later divided up responsibilities.

Detailed suggestions from the participants can save a lot of time. In order for this to happen, all the participants should get an agenda with explanations well in advance of the meeting. Some Quakers avoid taking prepared suggestions with them to a meeting because of the risk that you might not want to let go of them later. I think this is underestimating yourself and others.

In the summer of 1988, I participated in a long gathering on civil disobedience. Two days were wasted as the fifty participants discussed all kinds of practical and organizational questions. In a passion for direct democracy, *planning* and *decisionmaking* was mixed up. Meetings are a bad forum for detail-planning. On the other hand, they are of course quite good for discussing and making decisions on different *suggestions*.

Many other tools besides the ones mentioned above are used (including some I will go into in the following sections). In Syracuse, a secretary always wrote down **summaries of all of our contributions**. Otherwise it is more common to record only the decisions that are made.

A useful and interesting method that can be used in large group discussions to stop some participants from dominating comes from the North American Indian tradition. The person who has the floor holds a **speaker's stick** in his or her hand. When other people want to say something, they have to ask for the speaker's stick from the person who spoke last.

An old tool that can be useful in decisionmaking that is often forgotten these days is **silence**. At important discussions in our Pershing Plowshares group we were silent for a moment between each speaker. We did this for several reasons. First, we could really concentrate on the person who was speaking without having to think at the same time about what we were going to say. This meant that we didn't have the feeling that you have to repeat what has just been said so that the others will really understand. This saved a lot of time. The moments of silence also gave us the opportunity to think for a while. In this way the contributions that followed were based on previous reflections, like Socrates' dialectical way of discussing. That is not the case when you have ready-made opinions and the right to speak goes back and forth between a few people until one side has won. Silence provided time to relate the discussion to our goals. It increased both concentration on the subject and our ability to survey the situation.

Silence can be useful even in discussions that are not that important. A Quaker once told me that her meeting usually had a few seconds of silence after each speaker to avoid people's interrupting when the speakers were just taking a deep breath or had lost the thread of what they were saying. Quakers usually have a long period of silence at the beginning and end of their meetings. This probably also increases concentration on the overall goals.

Facilitators

The role of chairperson has been heavily criticized. It is both a source of uneven distribution of power and a job that is very difficult to carry out well. It is almost impossible to find a chairperson that can manage the entire responsibility placed on her or him. In order to achieve a higher and more even quality level at meetings, several progressive movements in the U.S. and Europe have changed the function of the chair and divided it up among three and sometimes even four people. So as not to confuse these roles with the traditional role of the chairperson, new names are used, like: **facilitators,**

vibe-watchers, sexism-watchers, process facilitators and **timekeepers**.

The **facilitator** leads the meeting, makes sure that everyone gets a chance to speak, and keeps the discussion to the point and on the subject at hand. This person tries to get the discussion to develop in a constructive way. Often the facilitator has to interrupt the discussion because someone is repeating him- or herself or happens to break off a round that is in progress.

If a decision is to be made, the facilitator can move the discussion forward by summarizing the recommendations that have been made now and then.

The **vibe-watcher** is one of the roles designed to lighten the load of the facilitation. This person brings out into the open hidden or underlying conflicts, mediates, and helps silent or weak minorities to be heard. A typical job is to interrupt the discussion for a pause when it has run into a dead end. An experienced vibe-watcher can even articulate things that are going on under the surface of the meeting that the participants aren't really aware of. One thing that happens a lot is that men often discuss things with each other and perhaps look for support from the women. By observing the participants' eye contact, the vibe-watcher can see if some people are running the show while others are on the periphery. In the European Plowshares, we have started to use a **sexism-watcher** to complement the vibe-watcher.

At more difficult meetings of bigger groups, a **process facilitator** might be needed. This person also complements the vibe-watcher and takes over the responsibilities that have to do with keeping democracy functioning. The process facilitator can make suggestions that have to do with the process of the meeting, like the need for dividing up into smaller groups, letting a committee rework incomplete recommendations, or quite simply pointing out that the group does not have the right to make a decision about a certain question if not everybody is present.

Of course, other participants can make suggestions about how problems with the process of the meeting can be solved. A practice used in large groups is that those who want to address points of order can raise both hands, then be placed at the top of the speaker list. This is equivalent to a point of order in the traditional meeting techniques.

Timekeepers are responsible for making sure that the time limits are kept and that the meeting ends when it is supposed to. During my first year in the U.S., I attended meetings several times a week. Just about every meeting ended at the time we had decided on beforehand; at the most we went five minutes over. This punctuality was perhaps not that strange since all the participants—except me—were used to this way of making decisions. Anyway, I felt surprised after each meeting that the level of stress didn't increase toward the end of the meeting. I was used to feeling stressed at meetings and I wasn't used to finishing on time. This lateness was a democratic problem because people had to leave, and more and more disappeared the longer we went on past the agreed time of conclusion.

One necessary condition allows the timekeeper to keep to the agreed-upon time limits. Every point on the agenda needs to have its own time limit. These are decided at the beginning of the meeting. They are then written beside the points on the agenda on an easel or a chalkboard so that everybody can see them.

What do you do if the time limits can't be kept? On one occasion my peace group in Syracuse was going to employ another person to work our printing press. We put aside half an hour to discuss this question. The next point we were to discuss was shoveling the wheelchair ramp during the winter. After fifteen minutes of discussing the new job, the timekeeper let us know that half of the time was up. Just before the time ran out we were informed that only three minutes were left. But we didn't feel that we were finished. We decided to put off discussing the wheelchair ramp until the next meeting, since it probably wouldn't snow for a while. In that way we got ten extra minutes that were originally set aside for the ramp.

The difference between a traditional meeting and this form is that the prioritizing is done consciously. Instead of the last questions getting less and less time, we quickly decided on new time limits. This meant that we had plenty of time to discuss the last questions.

Many groups seem to think that it is enough to choose people for these facilitator roles and then everything will take care of itself. But chaos soon sets in. A common difficulty that arises when a group starts using facilitators is that they are often not used to strictly structured meetings. Too often we do not dare to guide the meeting. In the groups I have participated in we have rotated these roles. Then everyone gets experience in the different functions and at the same time a new hierarchy is avoided.

Mediating

Mediation techniques are used more and more as tools for decisionmaking. They have ancient roots and the Bible tells us that they were widely used before Israel developed into a state under Saul's rule about one thousand years before Christ. At nonviolence courses we sometimes practice mediation techniques since peacekeepers and vibe-watchers need this skill. Mediation is also used before an action, during negotiations. In the U.S., I participated as an observer in a course for mediation volunteers. The mediation movement is nonprofit; if both people involved in a conflict want to, they can bring in a mediator without charge.

Mediation has a central place in the philosophy of nonviolence. It is an attempt to solve a conflict without oppression, that is, without one side forcing the other to follow their will. The goal of mediation always is to reach consensus.

In most affinity groups, conflicts arise. Implications, unfinished sentences, underlying meanings, and body language can reveal hidden conflicts. If these affect the work of the group, then they should be brought into the open by the vibe-watcher. Then the group has to decide if the conflict should be discussed during the meeting or in another context. If the vibe-watcher thinks that he or she can be neutral, then he or she is given the role of mediator. The vibe-watcher should not be afraid of guiding or concentrating the mediation process. Otherwise the participants risk straying into a general account of their feelings and disappointments in life.

The mediation can start with a round where everyone is given the chance to interpret the conflict and express what they feel about it. After clearing the air, the mediator helps the different sides to specify their own desires and analyze how these are in conflict with the opponent's. It is pretty common that certain facts are hidden in these discussions. If they are not too private, the mediator can bring them out into the open by asking direct questions.

The neutral people can of course make recommendations for solutions. If the atmosphere is charged or people reach a deadlock, you can do a brainstorm or a round where for a limited amount of time nobody is allowed to criticize the suggestions that are put forth. In order to avoid misunderstanding, all decisions that are made should be written down. When all sides have agreed and the agreement has been put in writing, then the mediation process itself is evaluated.

I have described above how you can use mediation to solve conflicts at meetings and in groups. In the face of more difficult conflicts a deeper mediation process is needed than what can be organized in the middle of a meeting. Then you need several hours and sometimes several meetings that are intended only for solving the conflict. Here are some tips for a more systematic mediation. The mediation itself can be divided up into the following points:

- Have the mediator explain her or his role and how the process works.
- Find out the facts and the aim of the mediation process.
- Ask for suggestions.
- Negotiate.
- Make a written agreement.
- Find out if the notes from the meeting should be destroyed. This is especially important when dealing with private conflicts.
- Evaluate.

The precondition for mediation is that both sides want the help of a mediator. The goal is to arrive at a written agreement.

First you write down the aims of the different sides. It is important to keep minutes and write down your understanding as mediator of the conflict. In this way the conflict becomes structured. A good idea is to divide the conflict into a set of smaller problems and solve one at a time. Some questions might not have to be solved during the mediation process, but take a minute to decide when they will be dealt with.

Then make a list of what is standing in the way of a solution. Be aware of the fact that both sides can tend to withhold information, both from the mediator and from the opponent. Talk with each side alone, if necessary. This can be useful when one side wants to say something that it does not want to become generally known.

The mediator should be neutral. One side may try to win the mediator over. If the other side notices then it can retreat or lose confidence in the mediator. This can, of course, be avoided if you are aware of the danger.

Read aloud or summarize the recommendations now and then. This can create more of an objective distance on both sides and help them to see things more clearly. A summary can also help everybody keep track of the facts and recommendations that have been discussed. If one side is at a disadvantage the mediator can support them by referring to what they have said. It is easier to listen to the mediator than the opponent.

Suggest your own ideas for solutions or partial solutions. Just remember not to openly support a suggestion. Guide both sides so that they keep to the subject and feel inspired to suggest solutions. Often the biggest obstacle to a solution is that the mediator doesn't dare to really guide the process.

Consensus

Consensus usually means unanimity of opinions. As a method of decisionmaking, consensus is something entirely different. It is a way of making decisions in agreement. This should not be confused with unanimous decisions, where nobody is opposed. The starting point is that the whole group makes a decision together that everybody can accept. But that does not mean that everybody has to think it was the best possible decision.

Decisions by consensus probably have a more ancient tradition than the Greek experiments in democracy. Several North American Indian tribes still make decisions based on agreement, and have done so as long as they can remember. Many African cultures also are said to have used this form of advanced democracy. Refugees from Southeast Asia have told me about how decision by consensus is a part of their tradition. To what degree and how far back in time, I do not know.

In the industrialized world, the Quakers are the most well-known example of consensus democracy. They have more than three hundred years of experience. In the same way as the nonviolence movement in India, Quakers see the decisionmaking process as a search for truth. In this case, truth is nothing subjective or relative, but objective, and something all the participants can arrive at through discussion and reflection. The Quakers base this search on a beautiful thought that one of their founders, George Fox, formulated in the mid-1600s. He said that God is in each and every one of us. When they meet to search for the truth, they expect to find expressions of God in each other. Younger Quakers are often more pessimistic about the goodness of people and the possibility of seeing the truth.

Even if most people that work with resistance do not have the Quakers' perspective, a discussion about what we base our decisions on is essential, and I'd like to discuss it here at some length. Otherwise it becomes difficult to assert that the opponent is wrong and that we are right. The search for truth arises from the needs of the oppressed. The foundation of nonviolence and all political action must always be the needs of the poor. To work, as liberalism does, for the greatest possible happiness, for the greatest number of people is a dangerous perspective. The final consequence of this is a defense of the majority's oppression of the minorities. The majority's capture of political power from the privileged minority was necessary and a good thing. It was, however, not a final goal but a step forward on the road to a true life where we "set the oppressed free and break every yoke."[47]

Crucially, if we see the decisionmaking process as a search for truth, we don't stop at the question of what is best for the majority or even, as with consensus, what is best for all participants. Instead, we look outside the group and ask what the needs of the most needy are. And how, moreover, do we participate in oppression and destruction? At the risk of being accused of either objectivism or subjectivism where *humans are the measure of all things*, I maintain that you can see discussion as a way of coming closer to the truth. During the eighties, the German social-philosophers Habermas and Apel discussed consensus as the base for our ethics. When we use language, there is a built-in tendency to try to reach an agreement. Decision by consensus provides the foundation for a morality based on public interest. Their prerequisite is an ideal rational discussion without power, among all concerned. As a feminist I miss the inclusion of emotions; the practical process of reaching an agreement might require that the participants consider feelings. Maybe you could call this intersubjectivism.[48]

The transformation of nature can also be seen as a way of reaching the truth, as Marx thought, which is why he saw the workers as representatives of the truth. This is a perspective from the ground up. But it excludes the people who have the worst conditions—the unemployed and the outcasts.

Gandhi stated that resistance is a way to search for truth. He derived truth from being. Truth is therefore latent in every one of us. In order to reach the truth, Gandhi continued, a total devotion to "being" or "truth" is necessary. It is also necessary that we become "indifferent" toward all other interests in life.[49] If we do something wrong in spite of our devotion, then this will be automatically corrected afterwards.

Even though he stated that nobody can know the truth, Gandhi punctured his own philosophy at this point. There is nothing to support the theory that devotion to or belief in truth can in the end lead us down the right path. This is overconfidence in the method. Nothing can guarantee that our mistakes will be corrected or that the *truth* will win in the end in a conflict as long as you have the right attitude or approach. The world is not that mechanical.

There is another danger with this outlook. Just as with Marx, it is very near to pointing out an elite that has more access to the truth than others do. Many people would probably not be up to searching for the truth. Gandhi left no room for cowardice or retreat. The truth is accessible to the devoted. But isn't a fanatic devoted? Madness doesn't become more true just because you believe in it. Truth does not arise from belief or passion. Even those with the weakest faith must have access to the truth.

In October 1989 during a meeting in Haarlem, outside of Amsterdam, I discussed the question of truth with Phil Berrigan, who helped to start the Plowshares movement. He defined the truth as the totality of the right relationships between people and God, between one person and another, and between people and the creation. These relationships cannot be divided, but form a whole. Based on this definition, he wanted to show that "truth" is to serve your neighbor in the best way possible. Your neighbor is an image of God, and therefore a brother or sister. This servitude is impossible without a preservation of creation. Phil thinks that what stops us from seeing reality clearly and arriving at the truth is the gap between reality and our understanding of it, the gap between our understanding of reality and our way of expressing this understanding in words, and the gap between these words and the actions that express the words.

One difficulty that arises from Phil Berrigan's reasoning has to do with the question of who God is. According to his definition, God fills two concrete functions: to show people's kinship with each other, and to show that our sisters and brothers have a value and therefore we should serve them. Many people, however, would like to recognize human value even without God. In that case, the divine aspect could be removed from the definition. But God is probably more than a father and mother for Phil Berrigan. The definition of God is something more than human value. Unfortunately, we did not have time to discuss this in more detail.

It is, of course, possible to find weaknesses in all of the outlooks of these searchers for truth, but they present interesting perspectives. None of them seeks knowledge from disinterested observation, like the ancient objectivists who differentiated between the question of establishing facts and our will to know how we should act. This kind of neutral disinterest has been raised to an ideal today. Scientists, teachers, and journalists are more trusted if they just tell "how it really is" without presenting any values. There are, however, others who are trying to combine the questions of what is *true* and what is *right*. We should be able to emphasize the rights of the oppressed as opposed to the oppressor, and even maintain that these rights are true.

How can you say what is right? This question has been discussed at great length with judges and prosecuting attorneys at trials. During my time in prison in the U.S., this was one of the most important topics of conversation with other Plowshares prisoners. We agreed on the foundation: the most should go to those that have the least, and the best possible to those that are in the worst situation. But we couldn't prove this theory in a completely convincing manner. The origins of ethics are perhaps impossible to identify philosophically. Truth then becomes a question of faith. We have to continue to state what we think is right; the alternative is destruction. The fact that we are among people means that we have a certain confidence in them. Otherwise, who would ever dare to turn her or his back on someone else?

In both feminism and pacifism, consensus is usually seen as one way among others to develop democracy. It is an attempt to help democracy through the crises that arise when it hasn't been able to meet the needs of the minorities. To clarify consensus, I usually divide it into two forms: the collectivistic and the individualistic-collectivistic.

The first form implies that the group is considered more important than the individual. An individual alone cannot stop a decision. Usually a certain number of participants, ten percent for example, are needed to block a decision.

The other form of consensus combines a strong collectivism with a strong individualism. Consensus is a group-oriented way of making a decision, but the group doesn't have the right to place itself above the individual, or vice versa. This might seem impossible to combine, but the attempt to combine them is the real aim of consensus, as I see it.

In this type of consensus, anyone has the right to *block* a decision. If everyone involved wants to make a decision anyway, then the discussion must continue until consensus prevails. If there is no time for discussion or if those that block the decision do not want to discuss anymore, others can *block the blockage*. This means that there is neither a *decision* nor an *obstacle*. Either those involved can do what they want or the group is divided up. It is, however, very unusual that somebody blocks a blockage, since the discussion usually continues after the first blockage until a solution that everybody can live with is found. This latter form of consensus, with the right to individual blocking, seems to be the most common form used by the nonviolence movement.

When I had just moved to the U.S., an activist named Christa Pranter took it upon herself to introduce me to different movements. I questioned everything and we had several heated debates on consensus. In several cases I could not come up with any objections. I especially remember when she made an interesting connection between civil disobedience and consensus. Civil disobedience fills the same function in society as blocking does in a meeting. Civil disobedience is the minority's possibility of *blocking* a decision. The idea is to reach agreement through a renewed dialogue. Even in the few cases where resistance has completely stopped an activity, it can still be seen as a part of the democratic process. The conditions are that the intent of the participants is to *block* a decision until an agreement has been reached. It is therefore misleading to dismiss all *effective* actions as being undemocratic. It isn't necessarily true that the participants want to dictate the decisions.

Consensus as a Method

There are many reasons for using consensus. A lot of people feel that it helps them to make better decisions, because consideration must be given to all opinions and objections. The decisions are gone through more thoroughly, which leads to greater participation. One problem with majority decisionmaking is that the decisions are often difficult to carry out since many people do not feel that the decisions are their own. Functioning consensus reduces the number of people that leave the group.

Consensus has become popular in groups that work with civil disobedience, partly because these groups plan actions that have serious consequences for the participants. A majority cannot decide in which ways the others in the group should risk being imprisoned.

Consensus is used when it is necessary to bring conflicts and problems into the open. In certain situations, decisionmaking methods that suppress conflicts, such as minority or majority rule, are used. At a short course in nonviolence and civil disobedience, the possibility hardly ever exists of satisfying all wishes. A course is often planned by a small group, and whoever wants to can participate!

Even the freedom of the individual to do what he or she wants is a form of democracy. When free choice doesn't affect somebody else, then it can often be the most practical form of democracy.

Consensus can be used only when everyone wants to use it. Sometimes people have thought that the method was so fantastic that they have tried to force it on others. They have kind of missed the point.

Consensus is easiest to use in groups of up to eight people where the participants have a common aim. The method is more difficult and more structured than traditional meeting techniques. It usually takes a certain period of trying, as much as a couple of years, before an inexperienced group succeeds in making it work well. When this experience has been built up, then it is possible to use consensus in relatively large groups. Quakers and feminists, who have used consensus for many years, often make decisions with several hundred participants.

When most people in the group master the technique, then it is pretty easy to introduce it to new members. Tensions can arise when facilitators interrupt a newcomer because she or he has broken a round or lost the thread of the conversation. I do not think that facilitators should avoid these conflicts due to misdirected kindness, because in the long run this just creates chaos and irritation.

Unfortunately, groups that have just started to use consensus sometimes use a simplified decisionmaking process that can cause the meetings to become boring and ineffective. To help avoid this, I will describe in more detail how to arrive at a decision.[50] Consensus decisionmaking can be summarized in seven points:

- Describe the problem that is to be solved and limit the discussion accordingly.

- Have a *suggestion round*, in which recommendations and opinions are stated.
- Provide time for free discussion.
- The facilitator summarizes the discussion in a suggestion.
- This suggestion is then tested in a *decision round*.
- If the suggestion is blocked, more time for discussion is provided or another time to solve the problem is decided upon.
- When the group has achieved consensus, read the suggestion out loud and ask if it is complete or if something needs to be added.

Often the discussion becomes problematically broad and people start discussing unnecessary details. Therefore, the problems to be solved must always be defined and the discussion thereby limited.

When the problem and its parameters have been agreed upon, then everybody should be allowed to make suggestions. The discussion should not begin until everybody has had a chance to say what she or he thinks. This *suggestion round* is probably the most important reason that consensus usually works faster than other forms of democracy. All suggestions and opinions are gone through thoroughly before the discussion begins. Without this round, the first person who speaks usually influences most of the discussion. After a while, somebody proposes another recommendation and this is discussed for a while. The discussion continues in this way until all the suggestions have been presented. If the suggestion round isn't done sloppily, then all the suggestions and objections are there from the beginning. This provides a more comprehensive and interesting discussion.

After the round, the floor is open for free discussion. If the round has worked right, then it should be enough to discuss and adjust any seemingly incompatible and controversial suggestions. When this has been done, the facilitator summarizes the discussion in *one suggestion*. This is sometimes called *synthesizing the discussion*. The Quakers say that the facilitator "reads" the meeting. If she or he is not able to do this then someone else is asked to give a summarized suggestion.

This suggestion is tested in another round called the *decision round*. Here the participants have the chance to propose counter-suggestions or additional suggestions. When these have been discussed by the whole group, then the facilitator makes a new suggestion, which is tested in a new round. The ideal situation is, of course, that everybody thinks that this suggestion is the best possible one. Sometimes people can say that they do not agree but that they do not want to hinder the group. It is important that their reservations be written into the minutes. Another possibility for those that do not want to block a decision is to not participate in making the decision. This is called *standing aside*.

When someone has strong reasons for thinking that the group should not make a certain decision, then she or he has a responsibility to block the suggestion. If someone who isn't at the meeting has presented her or his opinions beforehand, the person representing her or him at the meeting can block a decision. Usually people who are not present do not have the opportunity to block a decision. The possibility exists, however, of blocking a group's attempt *to make a decision* from the outside. Perhaps the group does not have the right to make a particular decision in the absence of certain people.

This happened in a peace group in the state of New York, for example. Our coordination group decided to start a total noncooperation with the FBI. They sharpened the decision and decided that nobody was allowed to talk to the federal police. Even if you try not to give any information, the FBI can analyze what you say and how you say it and thereby gain valuable information about our lifestyles, backgrounds, and ways of thinking. The coordination group thought that it would be dangerous if this information got out.

A few of us that participated in this peace group couldn't accept their suggestion. We were planning civil disobedience and might need to negotiate with the FBI in the future. Nevertheless, we could not reach a mutual agreement with the coordination group. We then made our own decision that they did not have the right to put themselves above our decision. Strangely enough this did not lead to a division. Our blocking of the coordination group's decision was actually civil disobedience and was not perceived as being especially threatening.

I think that one of the reasons that we did not reach consensus with the coordination group was misunderstanding. The discussion took place in our newspaper and via representatives. If we had organized a few meetings for everybody involved then we probably could have gotten a real dialogue going and been able to use the tools of democracy and mediation that make consensus possible.

When someone blocks a decision, then everyone is allowed to explain themselves in detail. It is important to provide everyone with enough time to suggest solutions to the problem. If the group needs more information or more comprehensive suggestions, then the discussion should be put off until later. It can become hypothetical otherwise. When the discussion has run into a dead end it should also be broken off. In the groups I have participated in, we have used pauses, silence, or coffee breaks in order to later get a more fruitful talk going.

The group decides in advance what to do if consensus cannot be reached. This decision is called **fallback**. Quakers never make decisions without consensus. This means that the old decisions still apply until a new consensus can be reached.

Some groups vote and sometimes use a qualified majority. Some affinity groups in Germany have allowed the participants to just do whatever they want, which means that they have strong confidence in each other. To divide a group is a good alternative when the members are striving in different directions. We seldom have the courage to break up a group, because it is so often experienced as disintegration. If a group is divided in time, however, it can instead prevent a more painful schism later on. Blocking is not as common as one might think. After heated meetings, I have seen surprised participants ascertain that it was possible to finally reach an agreement.

A decision should be written down and read aloud to prevent misunderstandings and to avoid incomplete decisions. A decision usually consists of six components, which correspond to the following checklist:

- What action is to be done?
- How should it be performed?
- Who should carry out the decision?
- What is needed in order to carry out the decision? This should include information, material, support, etc.
- When should it be done?
- How will the group know that it has been done?

People often forget to include the last point, which is an automatic control, in the decision. Many good ideas come to nothing because of that. In my first affinity group, we chose a coordinator who was responsible for making sure that all decisions were carried out. When it was impossible for somebody to finish a job, the coordinator was responsible for finding someone else to do it. Or sometimes something did not get done simply because it was forgotten. The coordinator checked the status of each decision between meetings and so discovered if they had been forgotten.

When a consensus decision is to be made, many participants would rather not use large group discussions since usually only a few people get the chance to talk. Not only that, the discussions become much too superficial and incoherent. The solution is to find a way of working where the participants discuss in small groups for the whole time. One method, which can even be used right in the middle of actions, is called the **fishbowl** model. When a problem arises and all the information has been presented to everyone, the affinity groups meet alone. Each group discusses until it reaches a consensus. They then choose a representative, who becomes part of the fishbowl. The group of representatives sits in such a way that the other participants can hear them ("look into the fishbowl at them"). When they reach an agreement, the affinity groups are given the opportunity to discuss their recommendation. Someone then goes back to the representative groups with counter-suggestions if there are any. Discussions between the affinity groups and the representative group are alternated until there is a suggestion that everybody can accept.

Consensus in the fishbowl form is so difficult that it can hardly function unless most of the participants have experience in decision by consensus. A well-known example of negotiations in fishbowl form was when the newly established Polish union Solidarity negotiated with the authorities at the beginning of the eighties. These negotiations were sometimes amplified on speakers and even broadcasted on the radio.

Closed negotiations, such as salary talks, tend to obstruct participation and democracy. The hierarchy is strengthened instead. Consensus, on the other hand, assumes openness, just like civil disobedience. Openness is a condition for democracy. There is no guarantee, however, that decisionmaking based on participation, openness, and the possibility to block really provides the best decisions. Even if democracy seems to be working, *lukewarm consensus* can be the result, that is, a decision that is not largely supported. This can be caused by the facilitator's forcing the decisionmaking process, for example. It can also be a result of the classical problem that two incompatible recommendations lead to a compromise that nobody really thinks is any good.

The fact that this latter can happen in majority decisionmaking is perhaps not that strange. These dynamics are built into the necessity of pairing up suggestions against each other. If there are more than two suggestions, then the traditional counter-proposition voting is used in majority democracy. The following example can perhaps illustrate this problem in the dynamics of majority decisionmaking. Two contradictory recommendations are supported by eighteen and nineteen people, respectively. Suddenly three neutral enthusiasts suggest that ominous compromise. The chairperson has a presentiment of what is going to happen, but leads the discussion to decision anyway.

Someone calls for a vote. The original recommendations happen in this case to be set against each other in the first vote. Three people pass and one of the recommendations wins by one vote. The chairperson, who now knows exactly what is going to happen, reluctantly sets the winning recommendation against the compromise. The eighteen people that lost in the first round vote for the compromise since it isn't quite as hateful as the other recommendation.

The result: the compromise wins and we have three happy and thirty-seven bewildered participants in the meeting.

This shouldn't happen with consensus; the starting point, when confronted with two contradictory recommendations, is to find a third suggestion that is better than the first two. Bad compromises should be blocked. Unfortunately, the reality is not as beautiful as the theory. Most groups end up once in a while with lukewarm consensus. The only solution that I can suggest is that when we discover this dynamic in progress we take ourselves by the scruffs of our necks and block bad suggestions.

When the decisionmaking process is functioning poorly, either the meeting can become emotionally charged or the opposite can happen: nobody dares to block a decision. Sometimes people don't go to the meeting or keep quiet. Whenever this happens, the problem should be brought out into the open as soon as possible. Of course, then the difficulty of keeping out of the other ditch arises.

Resistance today is based on small groups that provide support for participants to deal with the consequences of actions. It is impossible to keep your private life completely outside of political work. A problem in newly started affinity groups is that the participants confuse the struggle for a better society with the struggle to solve personal problems. Indications of this are, say, when important reflections are constantly being interrupted by other discussions about disappointments in the group. Things work better if you ask yourself what you can give the group instead of what you can get out of it. It just leads to disappointment to expect the affinity group to function like therapy. It cannot, for example, improve an activist's bad relationship with her daughter. On the other hand, the relationship can affect the activist's ability to participate in resistance and it should probably be addressed from this perspective.

Good support demands that our fears of the consequences of resistance be dealt with. In order to keep calm during the action, we need to tell each other about how we have reacted before when confronted with other people's aggressions. And, of course, I am good friends with people in my affinity group as well. We have a lot in common and are mutually dependent on each other's support.

In an affinity group, it is not possible to always do what you *feel* like doing. Resistance is pretty hard and often quite boring. It also demands that conflicts be brought out into the open, and this can make you feel bad sometimes. The reason Quakers avoid making emotional statements before making decisions is probably due to similar problems. This matter-of-factness, however, is no solution for a resistance group that has to bring feelings out into the open in order to work through them. We do this not to develop ourselves, but because these feelings prevent us from acting.

It is not only the decisionmaking process and the behavior of the participants that decide how democracy will function. The type of organization is also important, especially when an affinity group cooperates with other affinity groups. The next section is about forms of organization for civil disobedience that are more effective than the traditional hierarchical ones.

Organization and Networks

In some cases anarchists have been totally opposed to organizations and organizing. Good deeds would happen spontaneously if the oppressive organizational structures didn't stop them. Alexander Berkman, an international revolutionary anarchist, who lived in many different countries since he was never granted asylum anywhere, thought that this was nonsense. He maintained instead that "organization is everything and everything is organization."[51]

There is a grain of truth in Berkman's simplistic, rhetorical statement. When I write this book, I organize my thoughts with the help of pictures and language. In the word processor, into which I am now staring, the electrical impulses are organized by microscopic threads, which are organized on chips. The word processing program that I am using, one of the most advanced on the free market right now, is just an organization of ones and zeros. Organization provides us with a set of possibilities. To organize is to change these possibilities.

Usually, we think more about organizing people than about organizing matter. If we organize matter in a better way, then we can create less-expensive housing or more environmentally compatible transport systems. We can even prevent matter from being used—for example, by putting ourselves in the way or by simply destroying the organization of matter.

Organization is a medium that communicates a message and can even realize this message. It is a prerequisite as well as an obstacle for change. When we work politically, we are trying to solve organizational problems but we also struggle for and against other people's interests and actions. Organization isn't, as Berkman stated, *everything*. It has its limitations. As an ex-customer of the prison system, I am glad that it does. I was affected by imprisonment but I never allowed myself to become completely subdued.

Organization is an aid—a tool that, when it restricts us too much, must be changed or destroyed. An affinity group is an example of the development of organizational forms. During the past twenty years, the forms of organization in the nonviolent resistance movement have changed dramatically. In 1972, the Danish group Never War Again, the Norwegian group People's Revolution Against War, and the Conscientious Objectors Central Organization in Sweden published a common handbook. According to this handbook, "the working committee established the rules" for actions. The following is from an outline for action discipline: "We agree with the rule that every action has a leader, and agree to carry out the intentions of the leader even on occasions when we perhaps cannot completely agree with *him* or understand *his* decisions." I have added the emphasis just in case somebody may have missed the gender. These days affinity groups plan and carry out the actions, not leaders, though conflicts can and do of course arise anyway.

To avoid large group discussions, coordination groups are used in connection with mass actions. At an action against Seneca Army Depot in New York State in 1983, we numbered about one hundred affinity groups. The organizations that had taken the initiative were responsible for starting a coordination group. This group kept in contact with the affinity groups and coordinated all the recommendations. Whoever wanted to affect a decision was allowed to attend the meetings. All decisions were made by consensus. The coordination group did not have power over the affinity groups and one affinity group could not decide over the other groups. The kinds of jobs assigned to the coordination group included establishing time frames and defining a common goal and guidelines for the action. Several coordination groups were established to deal with the practical details, like toilets at the site of the action, communication between affinity groups, and negotiations with the police before the action.

In the Plowshares movement we do not use coordination groups. In the U.S. movement, the Atlantic Life Community instead organizes retreats once every six months. At these retreats, participants from different groups can evaluate Plowshares actions, discuss political needs, or coordinate different activities. In Europe, the movement is not that established. Since the end of the eighties we have tried to organize so-called Hope and Resistance Retreats for everyone who is interested. Without constant contact among the groups, we lose the character of a movement. A movement has certain dynamics that an isolated affinity group doesn't.

In order to develop resistance, a more comprehensive discussion than what goes on in small affinity groups is necessary. Every new affinity group should be able to build on—or break away from—earlier experiences. The movement functions as a support, but at the same time, by providing thorough criticism based on experience, it can prevent an affinity group from losing perspective. The movement has also cleared the way for new actions. The dialogue has already been started.

In a locally intensive resistance where the affinity groups are involved in different problems, the need for coordination is greater than in the Plowshares movement. I was employed with a peace group in Syracuse, New York for eight months. It functioned at the time as a network of groups that worked with Indian rights, solidarity with Central America, refusal to pay military taxes, conscientious objection to military service, and gender equity. We seven employees provided service to all of these groups. Two groups coordinated the work. One of the groups was responsible for economic questions, the group's building, and the employees. The other group concentrated on ideological questions and activities. Neither of these groups had its own projects. If you wanted to have something done, you had to join an existing action group or start a new one.

The coordination groups' members were not elected: those that wanted to were given the opportunity to participate. If someone who was not a member of the groups felt that she or he was especially involved in a question, then she or he could participate when the question was discussed. That was the idea, anyway. I remember that conflicts arose when one of the coordination groups suddenly perceived itself as a board of directors with the right to direct. A few years later, other conflicts were said to have arisen when the coordination group responsible for activities was temporarily disbanded due to a lack of members. Without a group that could solve conflicts, they started to accumulate.

I thought, however, that in general this form of organization functioned well. A big difference compared with many other alternative organizations was that so many people were active. In traveling around Scandinavia and giving courses in civil disobedience, I have noticed that in most solidarity, peace, and environmental groups just a few people on the boards of directors are active. Only during short, intensive periods do boards succeed in getting a lot of people involved.

Put simply, a coordination group is responsible for coordinating the activities that have already been started, while a board of directors is responsible for starting and governing activities. I believe the fact that local boards keep the activities going is one of the most serious bottlenecks in the alternative and solidarity movements. We have a way of working where typically members of the board call around and ask the support members to help distribute flyers on Friday, or to stuff envelopes on Monday. This strong collective of leaders causes, paradoxically, *activism* to become individualistic.

Usually, a large part of the work is "taking care of what a board has to take care of." If we allow the board to take over the activities then we can't ask for more. It is ineffective for one group to be responsible for many different kinds of activities. It also causes the members to hand over all responsibility to the leaders. If some members become disappointed because the organization doesn't do more, then they declare themselves incapable at the same time.

Why not let the activity decide how the organization should be structured? If there is no activity, then no coordination is necessary. If only a few people are active, then a special coordination group isn't necessary, either. Only with a lot of activity is there any reason to spend energy on coordinating this activity. If you start at the wrong end, the level of activity will never be especially high. It seems to me that a group of three people can easily get three more people involved but a group of six people has difficulties getting six more involved. Participation increases when the group is manageable. This might be one of the reasons that individual boards have trouble getting people involved, while the smaller groups in Syracuse activated hundreds of people week after week.

A good form of organization does not necessarily solve all problems; whatever form is chosen can be misused. During a trip to southern Latin America I was challenged by the activists there. They were very surprised that we had so many members in our alternative and solidarity groups. They got even more surprised when I told them that their groups seemed to be more active than ours. Even if they had only ten, thirty, or in some cases over a hundred members, they did very impressive work. They just couldn't afford the idea of passive members.

OPPRESSION

During the eighties, it was common for resistance groups to discuss and evaluate oppression. The discussions that have especially affected the groups that I have participated in have been about sexism, racism, minorities, and elitism. Some examples of insights that have radically changed the work of the affinity groups I was in are presented here.

Subtler forms of oppression are also important because of the necessity for affinity group members to support each other. An example of this sort of oppression in an affinity group is when a person gets a reputation for not being able to deal with responsibility, or when someone is always being harassed. These forms of oppression are reproduced and become institutionalized in the group. In other words, the oppression is constantly reinforced, so that if someone is harassed or criticized, giggles and comments from the rest of the group and an embarrassed smile from the person attacked are required.

It is assumed that the victim at most defends her- or himself against the accusations. The attempt to defend oneself becomes part of the game. A pattern is created that allows the oppression to take root in the group. It would be embarrassing if the victim openly questioned the reason for oppression. A friend of mine prevented a certain jargon against him from becoming cemented in the group by asking: "Why do you say mean things about me?" The guilty party felt embarrassed and foolish!

It is fear of making a mountain out of a molehill or of making a fool of oneself that prevents us from doing resistance against tendencies to gang up. Of course, many ways of being disobedient in the face of group pressure work. If you hear about slander or gossip, you can confront the guilty party directly. Or why not take it up when the whole group is gathered? It is important to react as fast as possible, before the pattern starts to be reproduced.

It can be helpful to determine who is reproducing oppression and how it is done. The people involved can usually be divided into three groups: the oppressors, the victims, and those who in practice support oppression by their behavior. All of these people are involved and reproduce oppression. Any of them can start doing resistance. It isn't self-evident that the oppressed will start first.

For many years the women's movement has been analyzing how oppression arises in small groups. My first encounter with feminism was a painful experience. A male role in leftist movements was typically that we were supposed to take hold of the discussion and solve the problems that were brought up. Which is why I, like a lot of other men, adopted feminism with my whole heart, solved the problem of gender roles, and proceeded to spend my time criticizing my sisters and brothers who had not come as far as I had. A few hits below the belt cured me of this delusion. I then joined a discussion group for men. Pretty soon I understood that an old religious practice would have to become my relationship to feminism. It starts with confession and then restoration by forgiveness.

When I moved to the U.S. in 1983, I was confronted by a somewhat different kind of feminism from what I was used to in Europe. I met a revolutionary women's movement that had been working for many years on solving different kinds of organizational problems. Using their revolutionary methods, they intended to fundamentally change the prevalent models of organization. They often created totally new types of organizations. In Europe, utopianism had a bad reputation because of past failures and authoritarian tendencies. In the U.S., the alternative movement was realizing one vision after another. The utopias were not allowed to become oppressive. Their dreams were not the final solutions. Utopia meant, rather, being able to create and change according to need. Representatives from the women's movement were involved in all the alternative projects, from credit unions to co-ops and land trusts that were governed by the inhabitants.

Every affinity group that I have participated in sooner or later has had to deal with gender inequality. These difficult discussions have been at the same time a way of settling up with old *answers* and *solutions*. Positing a differentiation between behavior and role, functions, and characteristics is helpful here. The debate during the sixties about sexism (special treatment due to gender) was too one-sided and dealt mostly with gender roles. It brought forward two solutions to the problem between men and women: a more even gender representation and the need to break out of our gender roles.

Professions that were dominated by one of the sexes were thought to need the characteristics that the opposite sex could provide. The solution was a more even distribution of the sexes, more female chiefs and politicians for example. This would create a softer and more caring society. It did not turn out like everybody had hoped it would. Women felt that it was necessary to play by the rules of the game in order to compete with men. Female politicians continued to support the arms race and participation in the oppression of the Third World.

Few people dared to let go of their positions. To be guided by one's conscience was too risky. The condition for creating justice is to dare to relinquish one's sense of security. The security of a position of power disciplined the wielders of power. The goal became to compromise and smooth things over. A basic truth was not understood. We can compromise only about our own interests; we cannot compromise with other people's lives or rights.

In the gender role discussions during the sixties, we were limited and controlled by our roles. Half of our personalities were undeveloped. By changing roles, we could become more whole. A man that stayed at home with the kids was thought to develop the female side of himself. Of course the househusband and the guy working at the nursery did change, but the power relations did not. Throwing off ingrained roles is just one of several prerequisites for creating gender equality.

These two solutions were incomplete. They concealed issues like resistance, historical changes, societal structures and functions, and power questions. They prevented us from seeing our own participation in other people's oppressive actions and from understanding how different kinds of oppression were intertwined. The solution does not lie only in changing roles. Power is a relationship. Relationships can last only if people maintain them. Resistance against sexism is above all a question of disobedience.

During the preparation for a disarmament camp in Sweden in 1992, we started to use several actions against sexism: leaving a meeting to start a new discussion in the next room; breaking a meeting with humorous actions, like pantomiming what had just happened; silent protests, like turning our backs or refusing to participate in big group discussions; and separate gatherings and meetings of women.[52] We also chose special action groups so that those who felt oppressed didn't have to do the actions alone.

Minorities

I wonder if there were any minorities before the ideal of democracy started to develop. The idea that something called the majority should make the decisions instead of something called the minority started to become established during the nineteenth century. This was necessary and a good thing, but the problem of minorities arose as a result. Could the majority abuse its newly won power? Pretty soon people realized that it could. This is still apparent today when one sees that people with handicaps can't use public transportation and that refugees are not allowed into the country.

Even within the nonviolence movement, minorities have difficulties. Problems can come from the outside or from within the affinity group. Minorities can be used to belittle an action. The mass media can *marginalize* the participants by calling them "youth" or "the unemployed." In action campaigns, there are several ways of avoiding this. The women in the Women's Peace Encampment at the Seneca Army Depot were called middle-class feminists by the newspapers. In response they suddenly did a Lady action. Limousine after limousine rolled up to the military depot's main entrance and female representatives of the upper class poured out. Their chauffeurs carefully folded their furs while the ladies calmly blocked the entrance to the base. A military police officer stared at them in amazement before he got himself together enough to ask a commanding officer for orders. At the Pershing II base in Mutlangen, Germany, this method has been used consistently. Senior citizen's blockades and children's actions have been followed by blockades by judges and prosecution attorneys. Ex-concentration camp prisoners and doctors have had their own actions as well.

The terms *ageism* and *classism* are equivalent to terms like racism and sexism. *Ageism* means actions or structures that treat age groups differently. A typical example in Scandinavia is the tendency within the alternative movement for middle-aged activists to let the "impatient" youth take over: "We really need a strong youth movement today, the way it was when we were out on the street...." It is also common to let those "fantastic" senior citizens that have so much time on their hands take over the long-term work. Other types of tensions can arise within affinity groups as well. A North American senior activist, Marjory Nelson, has often seen younger activists treat older women like surrogate mothers, due to the stereotype of older women being sexless, considerate, and quiet about their own needs. Young women sometimes use older women to solve conflicts with their mothers.[53]

Classism is not the same thing as the struggle between the classes in society. This term is used more concretely to mean excluding people that belong to other classes in society from participation on equal conditions. The alternative movement is almost completely dominated by the middle class. This means that middle-class interests are somehow mirrored in the language, behavior, values, perspectives, and directions of the movement. Since the middle class also dominates on a cultural level and is the most numerous class in our society, a false impression can arise that all movements that work with peace and environmental questions represent the interests of the general public: "Everybody loses in a war," and "Who doesn't want a better environment?"

Many groups try to counteract this by starting coalitions that plan actions. By cooperating with unions, churches, social institutions, or interest groups like the disabled people's movement, the alternative movement forces itself to work with issues that might otherwise be forgotten. One example, the Campaign for Work and Peace in the U.S., was a cooperation between the unions and the peace movement.

For eight months, I lived in a Black ghetto with Patricia Narciso and Scott Rains. Scott was in a wheelchair after a spinal operation in his early teens. The constant crashes between Swedish and American, Black and white, male and female, Protestant and Catholic, middle class and working class, intellectual and illiterate, and mobility and disability made this an excellent place for me to become a little more aware of my own prejudices. The first thing I had to work through was that I did not want to admit that I had prejudices about disabilities. Then I discovered that disabled people also had prejudices, about other disabled people.

In the beginning I had a somewhat peculiar, good-hearted idea that Scott, in spite of his wheelchair, should always be *allowed* to participate. That was before I understood that Scott was one of the leaders in the peace movement and it was more the other way around, that other people got to participate on his initiative.

When I was arrested for the first time in the U.S., I was with Scott and Patti. I was tempted to see Scott as a hero and I thought that he should be put in the limelight. I also had the apparently contradictory idea that I needed to protect him. When Scott and I talked about these issues, he told me about other prejudices that were common. Many people thought that they couldn't laugh at disabled people when they made fools of themselves: "As though we cripples didn't have a sense of humor." He also talked about how hard it was to make eye contact with people. This is especially important in civil disobedience since it is a prerequisite for establishing contact.

In New York, the disabled activists do an interesting type of action, which should really be pretty self-evident. They try to live just like everybody else. This means that they do blockades every day when they try to get through narrow doors, use the subway, or make it to the perfume department one floor up.

When I lived in Syracuse, some people in wheelchairs started to plan blockades of buses and restaurants that were not designed for wheelchairs. I was surprised that Scott only reluctantly participated in their actions. He perceived himself as a peace activist. He worked with resistance against militarism. He wasn't a disabled issues activist. It was the rest of us that tried to put him into that category.

Scott tried to make it possible for disabled activists *to be able to* struggle against the military. For instance, the planning meetings for civil disobedience were held in buildings with ramps. Broader practical problems in connection with actions needed to be solved, like functional toilets, sign language interpreters, speakers, and food for diabetics. Many of these problems could be solved thanks to the system of affinity groups. Disabled people are stopped from participating in civil disobedience by the anxiety that their needs cannot be met. Taking their needs into consideration is an indication that they are welcome. This is also important at actions where nobody expects disabled activists to participate; the actions become a challenge to them to participate next time.

Other groups also have to struggle against prejudices within the nonviolence movement. Homophobia—fear of the same sex—is deeply rooted in our culture. It strictly controls our ways of socializing with each other. Homophobia can obstruct us in our contacts with people of the same sex. It creates oppression of people who do not take on the prevailing gender roles, such as women who are considered masculine and men who are considered feminine. It also strengthens the idea of the heterosexual couple as "normal," thereby implying also that people who are *alone* don't fit in. And most basically, homophobia causes oppression of lesbians, gay men, and bisexuals.

Bobbo, an activist friend of mine, wondered at a nonviolence camp why people would rather demonstrate for Black people's rights in South Africa with ANC (African National Congress) representatives than with lesbians and gay men for their rights here at home. "It is probably," she concluded, "because nobody suspects us of being Black even if we mix with them." There is some truth to her speculation. It is easy for us to be radical as long as we do not risk being oppressed ourselves.

During my time in prison I discovered one of the reasons for the effective racial segregation there. White prisoners didn't dare to hang out with Black prisoners because they were afraid that the others would suspect them of being homosexual. Black people were considered homosexual. This prejudice affected those of us who did hang out with them. This combination of racism and homophobia created a very strong segregation. To my dismay, I noticed that I even started to avoid bodily contact when I was together with Black people in prison.

Homophobia is a sensitive subject that often creates conflicts during nonviolence courses. Nobody—not even lesbians and gays—can claim to be free from this phobia. As long as a risk of conflicts continues it is an important issue to deal with.

Elitism

The word *elite* comes from the Latin word *eligere,* which means to select. It is used in the sense of the chosen, the best, the central group, or the vanguard. In resistance movements the risk of elitism comes from the belief in experience or spiritual and moral maturity. It can even be due to hierarchical decisionmaking.

Incomplete preparations or the absence of affinity groups can cause those that do not have experience to not dare to participate. It can also cause the formation of a central group of experienced and charismatic leaders. A recent study showed that informal or half-formal leaders can appear under such circumstances. These leaders ran the meetings before actions, standing out as leaders because they talked more than the others and people listened to them more. During actions, some of them tended to give orders. When participants turned to them and asked them directly for advice, however, the leaders emphasized that everyone had to make up their own minds what to do. Other people acted like these leaders, but the group did not give them the same status and ignored their orders.

An effective way to make a movement passive is to select heroes. A variation of this is to emphasize a vanguard or to talk about the spearhead model of resistance. The first person in my circle of friends that did civil disobedience was David "Chains" Karlsson. He said that when people are placed on a pedestal, their actions are considered to be above and beyond anything that we mortals can do. (He was given the nickname "Chains" because at that first action he chained himself to the gates outside of a nuclear power plant to stop a waste transport.)

The seventies and eighties were characterized by a settling up with elitism in the nonviolence movement. Along with criticism from feminism, the self-criticism within the left has affected nonviolence groups.

A point of common interest between the left movements and the nonviolence traditions has been the struggle for the oppressed. The Indian independence movement demanded equal rights for the casteless, for example, and Marxism emphasized the working class as representatives of the public interest. But who exactly are "the oppressed"? In the *Communist Manifesto*, Marx and Engels state that when the working class becomes aware of its existence as a class, it will become *the* revolutionary force in the capitalist society (my emphasis). This is questioned by the left today.

In 1984, Habermas wrote that our historical experience has shown us that "there are no clearly identifiable classes or social strata that in all cases allow themselves to be pointed out as representatives of violated public interest."[54] This criticism of Marx must also affect those that see women, Black people, or the lower classes as *the* "revolutionary" groups in society. Most people within the left seem to have been aware of Habermas's observations quite early on. History has shown that, generally speaking, women, workers, or the unemployed are not consistently radical or especially interested in representing the public interest, though a group can of course have a leadership role during certain periods of time.

The Leninist revolutionaries tried to solve this problem by appointing elites that represented the working class during the revolution. Their job was to train the workers to be conscious revolutionaries. As a result, the party elite led the revolution. With oppression and strict control they tried to educate the people. Diaries and biographies from this period tell of how Trotsky and Lenin were responsible for purging dissident socialists, anarchists, and liberals long before Stalin came into power.

Even the social democratic movement established the *party* in a leadership and governing function. Together with the communists, liberals, and conservatives, the social democratic parties have built up a strong state power in some countries. Parliamentarians and representatives of the government are thought to have a wider overview than the voters. They supposedly also understand the needs of society better than the nongovernmental grassroots movements. Local movements are run over time and time again in the name of the *public interest*.

Elitism has also developed in some leftist sects. In Germany, the urban guerrilla groups tried to make people understand capitalism's "true nature" by provoking more oppression. This tactic was also based on the assumption that an elite knew best and could therefore lead the people. But terrorism strengthened the people's support of the state control apparatus. The more violent the guerrilla was, the more support for increased control. The leftist sects in practice did the job for the political right.

These experiences provide many insights. We risk deceiving ourselves and others if we think that we can represent the public interest based on exclusive insights. In the same way, we can obscure reality if we think that we represent the poor and oppressed. It is impossible to really understand what it means to be poor without actually being poor.

In the industrialized world we are, of course, also oppressed in different ways. We can talk about our own liberation. This can mean liberation for the unemployed and women, or freedom from poisoned air. There is a danger in seeing oneself as a liberator of others.

A North American pastor who moved into a slum reflected over this issue.[55] Jim Wallis was cured there of the illusion that he could identify himself with the poor and that he could help them. Daily contact with the poor is necessary, however, in order to understand how we are oppressors ourselves. We need to be reminded of this on a regular basis. This daily contact challenged him to start a struggle to reduce our mutual oppression instead. Those of us in the middle class need to move into areas where the people with the most difficult circumstances live.

Cooperation with oppressed groups cannot be based on the poor's need for us to represent them. Contact is, however, important, since it creates a dialogue that can lead to mutual decisions and continued cooperation. The struggle to reduce our own oppression is confronted with the struggle for liberation. But the Third World's liberation ideologies cannot be taken over. At best, this struggle leads to a continued cooperation and the dialogue challenges us to escalate the struggle against our own contributions to oppression.

One difference between leftist and nonviolence movements is that the latter, according to its tradition, doesn't necessarily defend the public interest. If, for example, we stop a corporation from exploiting the Third World, this could theoretically lead to a difficult economic situation in that country. Our struggle can defy what is considered to be in the public interest.

CHAPTER VIII

LEARNING RESISTANCE:
ABOUT TRAINING

THE HISTORY OF TRAINING

Civil disobedience isn't over just because the prison sentence has been served. It isn't over until a mutual solution to the problem has been reached. After the actions, training and preparation of new participants follows.

Education in civil disobedience has a long history. The mediators mentioned in the Old Testament solved conflicts before Israel became a kingdom. This *wisdom* must have been communicated by older judges. In the Far East, Buddhist monks were said to be trained in nonviolent defense methods as protection against thieves and robbers. Aikido and jujitsu might be developments of this tradition of nonviolence.

Gandhi used different kinds of training. He emphasized daily training of awareness, the body, and speech. This constant training is hard work and must be done even if you don't like it. The goal is self-control, with speech, awareness, and the body all coordinated. Given this tradition, it is understandable that Indian nonviolence training today includes everything from practical work to meditation and conversation. Their training is relatively long. The Institute for Total Revolution, for example, offers ten-month training programs.

The Institute is run by Narayan Desai, who grew up together with Gandhi in his ashrams. Narayan's father was Gandhi's secretary. In his book *Handbook for Satyagrahis*, Narayan discusses training in depth.[56] The satyagrahi is basically an active person. Action is more important than sermons or lectures. Satyagraha is, according to Gandhi, a method for public education, and a way of life that includes direct action. The satyagrahis prepare themselves for these actions by developing knowledge, activity, and devotion.

Narayan's handbook is interesting in that he presents a study of other people's criticisms as a way of developing his own knowledge about resistance. Understanding each other is a part of the solution. Habits and abilities are also knowledge. Reflexes can probably be considered knowledge, and can be trained.

Devotion and the willingness for self-sacrifice are more difficult to train. These are developed, according to Narayan, through a constant striving and humility. The prerequisite is to understand the oneness of and affinity between people.

Nonviolence training is well developed in India today. The struggle for independence started without training. After several failures, Gandhi emphasized the importance of all participants in civil disobedience receiving nonviolence training. After similar failures during the fifties, the civil rights movement in the U.S. came to the same conclusion.

Training in the Western world is somewhat shorter than in India. We think we can cover nonviolence during one weekend.... The United States is the Western country where training is used most consistently before actions. Often nobody is allowed to participate without having taken a course. In Germany, the same demand is often made, but in

Europe in general, training is not as well established as in the U.S. Based on experience from the 1980s, more and more people stress the importance of careful preparation. The problems that we have had with badly prepared activists or in some cases with provocateurs retard the development of resistance.

Training has changed over the years. During the 1970s, purely technical training was popular. The interest in civil disobedience was exchanged for an interest in direct actions: actions should be directly effective. Courses included training in techniques of how to lock arms, be dragged away, climb fences, and protect yourself against police dogs and tear gas.

Women from feminist groups in the U.S. began to participate more and more in civil disobedience from the mid-seventies on. These women confronted and questioned the male conscientious objector's interest in techniques. Resistance is for everybody, they said. Old women and young girls should also be able to participate. The young pacifists had to satisfy their male performance anxiety in other contexts—tug-of-war or ping-pong competitions, for example.

The *technique tradition* seems to be tenacious in Norway and Australia. In Norway, people become experts on chains, and in Australia tree-huggers have glued their hands together with superglue to stop the cutting of the rain forest. An interesting remnant of the "technique epoch" is the Swedish theater group Earth Circus, which has on different occasions trained affinity groups in acrobatics. In spite of the fact that acrobatics exclude many people, the anti-authority jester tradition can develop solid resistance.

The most well-known trainers during the seventies and eighties were Hildegard Goss-Mayr and Jean Goss.[57] For many years they traveled around the world, providing training in nonviolence. They trained people in the Philippines right before the peaceful revolution in 1986, and also led training in different authoritarian countries in Latin America. Their preparations consisted of three parts: conflict analysis, preparation of base groups, and the working out of a strategy. The analysis covered historical, ethical, ideological, political, legal, and pedagogical conditions, as well as traditions and culture. The group also analyzed what makes injustice possible. Which people, groups, and institutions are involved in the conflict? In which ways?

One of the fundamental questions for Jean and Hildegard was how all of us are jointly responsible for injustice. The nonviolence struggle can never put the entire blame on the opponent. This analysis is "bipolar." It attempts to embrace both the oppressed's and the "other side's" truths. It assumes that the opponent can in some ways be right. As the first instrument of resistance, this analysis gains its real importance. You can use it in discussions with the opponent during trials, for example, and with the public. During these discussions, the analysis is adjusted.

The base group's inner conviction is decisive for its strength and effectiveness. The feeling of solidarity and spiritual strength must be constantly renewed during the struggle. This is done by inner preparation. Hildegard and Jean stressed, just as Narayan Desai did, the need for education in self-sacrifice. A price must be paid if injustice is to be overcome—and this price must be paid by the nonviolence activist and not by the opponent. The stakes are professional and economic disadvantages, or prison, or losing one's life. This sacrifice frees the participants from their chains. It also frees the strength that makes it possible for the opponent to achieve a new and more righteous conduct. The resistance gives the opponent strength!

While this is a powerful idea, I think that the analogy with an exchange of commodities—a certain price that has to be paid—is unfortunate. Price is related to value. The price should in some way reflect what a commodity is worth, but the value of the punishment for civil disobedience does not in any way reflect the injustice that we are struggling against. The punishment cannot at all be compared with the injustice. Some people like being in prison and others do not. It is wrong to say that those who are executed or imprisoned during the struggle against the arms race, for example, pay the price of injustice. Today tens of thousands of children are dying of starvation. Tomorrow there will be thousands more. The arms race demands its victims before the weapons are even used. Nobody can pay a price for this suffering.

Solidarity, environmental, and peace work will mean that activists even in the Western world will be imprisoned and executed. If I may give a positive interpretation of Hildegard Goss-Mayr and Jean Goss, maybe they simply meant that the struggle will lead to risks and suffering. If we are not prepared to take the consequences, then we do not have any possibility of stopping the injustice.

The above is all about inner preparations. The base groups need outer preparations as well, according to Hildegard and Jean, such as training ourselves in controlling our reactions, thoughts, and actions. We should even prepare ourselves to face scorn and slander, physical and psychological violence.

Jean and Hildegard used meditation, fasts, relaxation exercises, and role-playing for this preparation. In role-playing, the participants imagine themselves in a typical situation, such as a dialogue or civil disobedience. The roles are divided up and played by the participants. The point is to try to put yourself in the opponent's situation, in their way of thinking and acting. Afterwards there is always an evaluation of the role-playing.

These trainers saw the cooperation in the base groups as training in nonviolence. We all need practice in the patience and caring that is needed in order to work together. Small daily events are also practice. Nonviolence is an attitude toward life.

The last stage in the training—working out a strategy—is completely dependent on the particular situation. The mainstay of the nonviolence struggle is dialogue. If the opponent breaks off the dialogue, then those concerned must, with the help of actions, see that it is resumed.

Dialogues can often consist of two monologues. Hildegard and Jean maintained that a real dialogue demands careful preparations. To facilitate this they divided a dialogue into four different steps:

- Discover the opponent's truth and show respect for them as people. The base group can emphasize the positive contributions that the opponent has made.
- Discover and admit your own contribution to the conflict. When you openly admit your own faults, this increases the possibilities of activating the consciences of the opponent. It challenges and provokes the opponent to admit that they are also responsible.
- Describe the injustice.
- Contribute constructive suggestions and solutions. The people concerned are responsible for finding solutions, which they present for discussion. It is important to show your own willingness to participate in the work.

If the discussion is broken off, then all four of these steps in the dialogue can be carried out with the help of actions. According to Hildegard Goss-Mayr and Jean Goss, direct action is a dialogue that is carried out in a public forum. Its aim is to complement the words and illustrate the injustice.

Other international trainers are also well known. The Norwegian farmer and president of War Resisters

International, Jörgen Johansen, consciously chooses to use more traditional teaching methods at his courses. He has criticized the use of role-playing, claiming that the participants are often inclined to confuse role-playing with reality. The best training, he says, is doing actions and working practically with nonviolence. Significantly, Johansen stresses the importance of not mixing up therapy and training. Deep, therapeutic exercises can cause serious damage if they are used in a superficial way. Jörgen Johansen is one of the few trainers that give courses in nonviolence for local union chapters. These courses are usually about five days long and are given during working hours.

More and more interest groups see civil disobedience as a part of their work. Andy Mager from the U.S. has held courses in civil disobedience for disabled people's organizations. I have held courses for different political parties, scouts, and even confirmation classes. In January 1988, Nestor Verdinelli, Henrik Frykberg, Stellan Vinthagen, and I were facilitators for a four-day course on how to hide refugees, held at the University of Gothenburg's college of social sciences.

In the U.S., a lot of training is not directly concentrated on civil disobedience. All over the country, courses are held in mediation techniques to educate volunteers in conflict resolution. Women's groups provide training in how to deal with male violence. Often people in slums or in working-class areas organize nonviolence training for people who want to solve problems in connection with the areas where they live. Even schools organize nonviolence training for their students.

The Alternatives to Violence Project has quite successfully trained prisoners that wanted to learn how to respond to violence with nonviolence.[58] Witness for Peace educated people who went to Nicaragua during the eighties and stayed in combat zones in an attempt to create peace.[59] Peace

Brigades International trains people that go to Guatemala and other countries to function as nonviolence bodyguards.

The predecessor to Peace Brigades International was called the World Peace Brigade for Non-Violent Action. They held Sweden's first course in nonviolence in 1962. I do not know of any earlier course in my country. It was two weeks long and trained nonviolence activists that were going to go to North Rhodesia. The participants had to learn about everything from tropical diseases to the country's cultural patterns. They studied the political background of the conflict there and prepared themselves for dealing with it with the help of socio-drama, which is a kind of role-playing.

Preparation for Nonviolence

At the beginning of the eighties the word *training* was criticized. It could fool you into thinking that you could just learn nonviolence by taking courses and that the trainers knew more about it than the participants. Hence, in the U.S., the concept of *preparation* is commonly used instead of training.

The goal of nonviolence training is to start a dialogue that can lead to decisions about resistance. My aim with each course is that by the end of the course all the participants will be able to train others. My ambition is that this will also actually happen. Another goal is that the participants build affinity groups.

The two main components in my nonviolence courses are discussions about resistance, and methods that can facilitate these discussions. The most important discussions are those about practical, ethical, and theoretical questions. I also use role-playing about possible situations, or exercises to help us analyze different problems.

Training tools are directed toward resistance and conflict resolution. They can be useful in organizing information or a campaign. Above all, they are used to increase understanding by clarifying or structuring problems. The tools for training should function as an introduction to a discussion. It wouldn't be a good idea to use role-playing as a training in techniques and skills. The role-playing itself does not provide any answers for how to do resistance. Role-playing applies generally and in principle; real resistance is concrete and specific. Every action has its own unique characteristics that no exercises or earlier experiences can predict. But it isn't helpful to just skip role-playing in an attempt to avoid the "this-is-how-it-is" mentality.

When the trainers just talk about earlier action experience, both the listeners and they themselves believe that the next action will happen in the same way. Hopefully, role-playing can give the participants a new perspective and sources for new ideas that can help them solve problems that arise at actions. This also allows the facilitators to leave their facilitator positions and learn something, too. The fact that role-playing is not true to reality is thus its strength.

All these tools should be used to fortify and strengthen the affinity group. I am very critical of the training that is sometimes done in Germany, where different exercises force unconscious aggressions or feelings of anxiety to the surface. The aim is probably to become aware of the violence inside us; the result, however, is that only those who are psychologically strong can participate in these exercises. The rest avoid them or are broken down by them.

The need for training varies. The basic idea is that we all need skills and agreements about how to function together. This training is useful for both the relationships within an affinity group and the activists' relationship to the opponent. Personally, I have a need for support to overcome my feelings of insecurity before an action.

Training also brings our traditions into the open. By learning from earlier experience resistance can be developed.

This conservative, traditional feature is the condition for a radical resistance.

Good examples of the necessity of training can be found by studying actions where some of the participants were not trained beforehand. The actions usually become dependent on the leaders. One group that used to be authority-oriented was the anarchists and syndicalists that did actions on Sweden's west coast during the eighties. They did a lot of successful actions against arms export and the use of herbicides along railways, like blockades of trains loaded with weapons or herbicides. The people who had earlier experience or had gone through the syndicalists' training became the leaders at the next action. The initiative to do an action was taken by a few people who were very experienced; the knowledge of how to work with affinity groups was never built up. It isn't always the fault of the leaders that they have too much power. Paradoxically, the leaders in the group in western Sweden strengthened their positions when they declared that everybody should decide for him- or herself and that there were no leaders.

Preparing a Course

When planning a course in civil disobedience, either the facilitator is chosen from the participants or someone from the outside is invited to hold it. The latter is probably the most common situation. If the participants themselves are to lead the course, then they can divide up the responsibility and each take one subject. Then everyone gets experience in training others.

There is a significant difference between a course that is a direct preparation for civil disobedience and a course that is held for people who just want to know more about it. During courses that do not have a concrete aim, the facilitators have to fight to make sure that the time spent at the course does not just provide intellectually stimulating entertainment.

Several facilitators try to counteract this tendency toward entertainment by scheduling time on the first day for planning. The goal can be to start affinity groups or start planning an action. The conflict that has to be solved here is that some people perhaps do not want to plan resistance. This problem can be avoided if the goal of the course is specified in the invitation.

Another solution is to adapt the course to everybody's interests. The most simple way of doing this is to divide the course into interest groups. It is common to hold several parallel *workshops* that deal with different subjects. In this way, those miserable, boring, large group meetings can be avoided. A *workshop* shouldn't have more than seven participants if the discussions are to function well. ˜

When I am responsible for a course for a group other than my own affinity group, I usually let the group choose the vibe-watcher and the timekeeper. Then the participants are also responsible for keeping everything running smoothly. Otherwise, the group tends to transfer the responsibility to the facilitators. So that the facilitators really take their responsibilities seriously, I usually make sure we have an evaluation of our jobs when half the course is over. This evaluation helps everyone to understand the point of having facilitators better than if I just explain why we usually use them.

Briefly, I maintain that the aim of a course is to bring out problems of using civil disobedience and then together with the participants try to find solutions. The problems can be violence or oppression in the society, power structures in the group, the participants' personal fears, or the difficulties with civil disobedience. These are brought into the open in different ways; it is common to combine group discussions, role-playing about possible situations, and short lectures.

A course in civil disobedience is not based on the facilitator's experience, but on the participants' uncertainties and apprehensions. Anyone who has asked him- or herself how paralyzing obedience can be overcome, and who can imagine some of the difficulties that might arise during an action, can hold a course.

CHAPTER IX

THE FUTURE OF RESISTANCE: ABOUT POSSIBILITIES

THOUGHTS ABOUT A DISOBEDIENT UTOPIA

"But what would happen if everybody did that...?"

Well, then we wouldn't have any environmental destruction or arms export. But that is just a dream, I guess. We are too obedient. Maybe we will come closer to this utopia, so that disobedience becomes a part of our daily lives. This is undeniably an original vision: a society based on disobedience.

A society like that could hardly be harmonious. The holy and placid would probably not feel at home. Put simply, it would be perfect for us failures and doubters, those of us that don't want tranquillity or to live in harmony with our neighbors. With our defects we would never be able to live in a problem-free society. We would soon be pointed out as being the problem.

On the other hand, I wouldn't want to live in chaos. Disobedience isn't meaningful without order. What would we be disobedient of? A society where we citizens took direct responsibility and came of age, politically speaking, would

205

have to be much better organized than the chaotic situation we have now. No matter how well organized it was, disobedience would still be necessary. Nobody is perfect. How, then, could our organizations be perfect?

Every society, be it a utopia, a parliamentary democracy, or a dictatorship, is going to have problems with obedience and power. Disobedience is necessary to break the concentration of power and make these societies a little more humane to live in. My vision is a mixture of a well-developed cooperation and a well-developed disobedience when the cooperation becomes oppressive.

Personally, I do not have any illusions about the essential goodness of people. On the other hand, I don't have any illusions about their essential evil, either. Failures are a part of our lives, but in spite of our failures a lot of good things happen. Now and then a person comes up to me and says something beautiful. Then I can't deny that which is good.

I would not be able to trust even myself if people started to obey me. I would become corrupt. Who can guarantee that I would provide good solutions? We can find good solutions only together. Only if you believe in a human being's unimpressionability and absolutely noble mind would you dare to give people as much power as many have now. Power doesn't just exist. We can't just take it if we want it. We create power through our obedience. We are responsible for corruption. In my dreams, disobedience is a part of the letter carrier's and the shop assistant's daily life. From professional education programs to courses for union members, disobedience is on the schedule.

To be a democratic citizen is to take responsibility for each other's actions and decisions, not just one's own. Disobedience would thus be directed not only at corporations or governments. Religious institutions also need to be confronted with disobedience. Even unions need disobedience from their members. I think that the Plowshares movement and the Sanctuary movement, for example, would gain from disobedience from their participants.

This disobedience needs meeting places, places where we can meet and discuss until we arrive at mutual decisions. Politics means organizing these meetings. Disobedience is to meet again when one side has refused to discuss and left the meeting place.

How do we achieve this? Are these dreams a far-off utopia? No—they are realized every time we take responsibility for each other. They are realized when we work together for a better life for everyone. This utopia can be realized each time someone refuses to obey an order that can hurt someone else.

But these dreams could realize much more than this.

To get there, grassroots organizations need to not just whine about and protest against the shortcomings of the authorities. Disobedience and mutual creativity should be the two most important activities. The obstinate whining could still be a part of this, I guess, but it shouldn't dominate to the great extent that it does now. In the long run who could stand to listen to such nagging? No—take a break from nagging! Be a little creative instead!

Now is the time for a revival, as they say in religious circles. Disobedience must become a part of our work, our political commitment, and our relationships to our neighbors. Don't turn your back. Turn around. Meet power face to face. Disobedience is a responsibility. But wouldn't it be nice to just let someone else take that responsibility! Or...!?

ACKNOWLEDGMENTS:
A HANDBOOK GROWS

Just as with other handbooks, this one is the result of innumerable more or less successful attempts to practice the subject. It has grown out of discussions and work mostly in the Plowshares movement and during courses in civil disobedience. People have read different versions of my manuscript and provided many concrete suggestions for changes.

I would like to especially thank the following people. Leif Herngren has read the different sections several times as soon as they were finished. "You have to rewrite this," was the general comment. Stellan Vinthagen, who is also a facilitator in civil disobedience, gave me several good suggestions. I also forced three friends of mine from the Department of History of Ideas at Gothenburg University—Amanda Peralta, David Karlsson, and Mats Andrén—to criticize my book. They have been very patient and gone through the book page by page. They turned around and forced me to polish the more theoretical sections. Unfortunately, I could not make them less controversial. It isn't really true that I "turn all conceptions upside down." I see myself as being pretty faithful to the tradition that I discuss.

The people who have read parts of the book have also been a great help. Birgitta Westlin only had to glance through the manuscript to give useful suggestions for improvement. I asked my friend Mats Hårsmar, who happens to be a journalist, to examine the section on mass media. A lawyer, Lennart Brodén, tidied up the chapter about trials. Ola Westlin, who is a teacher, generously looked more closely at the chapter on training. A solidarity worker from Peace Brigades International who is also a trainer in civil disobedience, Henrik Frykberg, gave me some suggestions about how the handbook could be more useful. The editor for the Swedish version, Ingela Palmquist, provided several important suggestions; so did the editor for the English version, Yvonne Keller. My translator, Margaret Rainey, suggested quite a few improvements. My American publisher, Martin Kelley, asked me to add some important parts in the English version.

I would also like to thank my Swedish publisher, Hans Isaksson. Without his support I would probably not have spent several years doing investigations and revising material.

NOTES

1. Thoreau, H.D., "Civil Disobedience," *The Selected Works of Thoreau*, Walter Harding, ed. (Boston: Houghton Mifflin Company, 1975).
2. Ibid., p. 796.
3. Gandhi, M.K., *Non-violent Resistance* (New York: Schocken Books, 1985), p. 18.
4. Thoreau, "Civil Disobedience," *Selected Works*, Harding, p. 795.
5. Rawls, J., *A Theory of Justice* (Cambridge, Massachusetts: The Belknap Press of Harvard University Press, 1971), pp. 333-391.
6. After World War II, certain principles for international law were established, known as the Nuremberg Principles. These principles apply to all citizens, not just official representatives of the society. According to these principles, if a government breaks international law, the citizens have a greater responsibility to obey the international law than to obey their own government. Otherwise, the citizens become accessories to the government's crime.
7. Gandhi, *Non-violent Resistance*, p. 38.
8. Ibid., p. 6.
9. Sharp, G., *The Politics of Nonviolent Action* (Boston: Porter Sargent Publishers, 1980; originally published 1973), especially Part One and Part Three.
10. Ibid.
11. Kropotkin, Petr, *Mutual Aid: A Factor of Evolution* (London: Freedom Press, 1987).
12. Unfortunately, I have been unable to find any literature where Phil Berrigan goes into detail about this point. In discussions, he has stated that community is both the goal and the foundation of

resistance. A Plowshares group usually begins by finding out what the members have in common. This process in itself creates a sense of community.

13. Gandhi, *Non-violent Resistance*, pp. 55, 52, 40.
14. Mahatma Gandhi called his autobiography *The Story of My Experiments with Truth* (Ahmedabad: Navajivan Publishing House, 1989; first edition 1927).
15. *Jane's All the World's Aircraft. Jane's Yearbook* (New York: Arco; published annually since 1929).
16. Wright, Peter, *Spy Catcher: The Candid Autobiography of a Senior Intelligence Officer* (New York: Dell, 1988).
17. Nyström, S., "Palmemord och affärer bakom säkerhets-boomen" (The murder of Palme and the business behind the security boom), *Veckans affärer* 37 (Stockholm, September 1988), pp. 86-89; and Britton, C., "Fler anställda än hos polisen" (More employees than the police), *Dagens Nyheter*, August 22, 1988.
18. Andersson, B.G., "Nye Säpochefen: Öppenhet ska ge nytt förtroende," *Dagens Nyheter*, September 21, 1989.
19. Agee, Philip, *Inside the Company: CIA Diary* (London: Allen Lane, 1975), pp. 35-97.
20. Ibid., p. 70.
21. Garrow, David J. *Bearing the Cross: Martin Luther King, Jr., and the Southern Christian Leadership Conference* (London: Jonathan Cape, 1988), pp. 281, 371-382.
22. Bratt, P., "Detta är Gunnar Ekberg..." (This is Gunnar Ekberg...), *Folket i Bild, Kulturfront* 10 (Stockholm, 1973), pp. 4-5.
23. Andersson, B.G., "Ansträngda US-relationer 1979, CIA avbröt Säposamarbete" (Strained U.S. relations 1979, CIA broke off cooperation with Säpo), *Dagens Nyheter*, September 24, 1989.
24. Davis, W.J., "Schemes and Devices, Surveillance," *Sojourners* 2 (1986), pp. 16-19.
25. Isa. 2:4.
26. Micah 4:4.
27. *Plowshares Newsletter* 1 (1988). P.O. Box 585, Orlando, FL 32802.
28. *The Nuclear Resister* 53, 54 (1988). P.O. Box 43383, Tucson, AZ 85733.
29. *Women's Encampment for a Future of Peace and Justice* (1983). 5440 Rt. 96, Romulus, NY 14541.
30. Hindenfeldt, C., *Arbetaren* (The Worker) 42 (October 21, 1988), p. 2.
31. Wellbring, C., *Arbetet* (Work), August 30, 1984.
32. Hasek, Jaroslav, *The Good Soldier Schweik* (Penguin Books, 1951).

33. Jensen, A., "Vad är sabotage: En undersökning" (What is sabotage: An investigation), (Ungsocialistiska Partiets Förlag (Young Socialist Party Publishers), 1912).
34. Ibid.
35. Foreman, Dave, and Bill Haywood, eds., *Expediences: A Field Guide to Monkeywrenching* (second edition) (California: Ned Ludd Books, 1987).
36. Clausewitz, Carl von, *On War* (Princeton, New Jersey: Princeton University Press, 1984; first published 1831), p.87.
37. Ricoeur, Paul, *The Conflict of Interpretations: Essays in Hermeneutics* (Evanston: Northwestern University Press, 1974; originally published 1969), p. 12.
38. Bergwall, P., "Ett helt dygns symfoni" (A day-long symphony), *Pax Tidningen för Fred* (Pax Magazine for Peace) 3 (1988), p. 9.
39. Wright, *Spy Catcher*.
40. Herngren, Per, *Plogbillsaktion Nr. 8* (Plowshares Number 8) (Stockholm: Bonniers, 1987). Not yet available in English.
41. Habermas, Jürgen, *Strukturwandel der Öffentlichkeit: Untersuchungen zu einer Kategorie der bürgerlichen Gesellschaft; mit einem Vorwort zur Neuauflage* (Frankfurt: Suhrkamp, 1991; first published 1961).
42. Kant, Immanuel, *Immanuel Kants Werke: Band IV*, Ernst Cassirer, ed. (Berlin), p. 363.
43. Thoreau, "Civil Disobedience," *Selected Works*, Harding, p. 798.
44. Gandhi, *Non-violent Resistance*, p. 66.
45. Gandhi, *Non-violent Resistance*, pp. 64-66.
46. Herngren, *Plogbillsaktion Nr. 8*.
47. Isa. 58:6.
48. Protagoras, who defined what we today call subjectivism in this way, lived 485-410 B.C.
49. Gandhi, *Non-violent Resistance*, p. 38.
50. See also Avery, M., et al., *Building United Judgement: A Handbook for Consensus Decision Making* (Madison, Wisconsin: The Center for Conflict Resolution, 1981).
51. Berkman, Alexander, *ABC of Anarchism* (London: Freedom Press, 1987; first published 1929), p. 53.
52. Herngren, Per, and Stellan Vinthagen, *Handbok Avrustningslägret i Linköping* (Handbook Disarmament Camp in Linköping) (Göteborg: Omega/Avrustningslägret, 1992), p. 27.
53. Nelson, Marjory, "Ageism." *International Day of Nuclear Disarmament* (1983), p.22. Livermore Action Group. 3126 Shattuck Ave., Berkeley, CA 94705.

54. Habermas, Jürgen, *Vorstudien und Ergänzungen zur Theorie des Kommunikativen Handelns* (Frankfurt: Suhrkamp, 1984), p. 479.
55. Wallis, Jim, *The Call to Conversion* (San Francisco: New HarperCollins, 1992).
56. Desai, Narayan, *Handbook for Satyagrahis* (Philadelphia: Movement for a New Society, 1980).
57. Goss, J., and H. Goss-Mayr, *Die Gewaltlosigkeit Jesu—eine Kraft, die Frieden schafft* (Jesus' Nonviolence—a Power that Creates Peace) (Düsseldorf: Bund der Deutschen Katholischen Jugend).
58. *Alternatives to Violence Project Manual: Basic Course* (1986). 15 Rutherford Pl., New York, NY 10003.
59. *Witness for Peace Training Manual* (third edition)(1986). P.O. Box 567, Durham, NC 27702.